Frequently Asked Antitrust Questions

Common Antitrust Questions Asked and Answered

SECTION OF ANTITRUST LAW

Section of Antitrust Law

This volume should be officially cited as:

ABA SECTION OF ANTITRUST LAW,
FREQUENTLY ASKED ANTITRUST QUESTIONS (2004)

Cover design by ABA Publishing.

Printed in the United States of America.

Library of Congress Control Number: 2004101834
ISBN: 1-59031-370-4

06 05 04 5 4 3 2

www.ababooks.com

CONTENTS

FOREWORD

The Section of Antitrust Law of the American Bar Association is pleased to publish this volume of *Frequently Asked Antitrust Questions*. This volume of *Frequently Asked Antitrust Questions* addresses a wide range of issues that lawyers, particularly in-house corporate counsel, face frequently. The publication also includes a resource at the end of each chapter for those looking for a more in-depth treatment of the covered subjects. Obviously, *Frequently Asked Antitrust Questions* is not a substitute for competent legal advice, but we hope that it will provide a quick introduction to the types of factors that in-house counsel need to consider when confronting antitrust issues in their daily practice.

Frequently Asked Antitrust Questions has been a publication that has been discussed for many years within the Section. It is the type of publication that we believe will be an essential part of any in-house counsel's antitrust library. I want to commend the current leadership of the Section's Corporate Counseling Committee for ensuring that this publication has been completed, but I also want to acknowledge the work of the immediate past co-chairs of the Committee, Alan Silverstein and Marcy Wilkov, for leading the effort to make this publication a reality. This was not an easy publication to prepare. I want to give particular thanks to Steven J. Cernak, Milton A. Marquis, and Michael B. Miller for their hard work in overseeing the team that did the actual drafting. The Section appreciates the experience, expertise, and effort that created this publication.

The Corporate Counseling Committee is one of the most active committees within the Section. It produces a large number of programs, newsletters, brown bag sessions, and listserv discussions. If you are not already a member of the Committee, I urge you to consider joining and becoming involved.

Kevin Grady
Chair, 2003–04
Section of Antitrust Law
American Bar Association

PREFACE

The Antitrust Section's Corporate Counseling Committee conceived of this volume as a helpful guide to those lawyers who are asked a wide range of antitrust questions, particularly internal counsel who are frequently asked questions by businesspeople looking for quick, clear and concise answers. *Frequently Asked Antitrust Questions* is designed for precisely those situations.

Many people provided valuable assistance to the creation of *Frequently Asked Antitrust Questions.* The initial drafting effort was led by Steven J. Cernak, ably assisted by a large number of Section and Committee members, including Stephen W. Armstrong, Christopher Dee, Nancy M. Lambert, Gil Ohana, Steve Ormond, Paula W. Render, Bilal Sayyed, Patrick M. Sheller, Richard J. Wegener, Dennis White, and Eugene F. Zelek. Former Committee Chair Alan L. Silverstein and Committee Vice-Chairs Milton A. Marquis and Michael B. Miller led the effort to finalize the drafting and to prepare the volume for publication. Thanks too to Dara J. Diomande and Jonathan M. Jacobson of the Books and Treatises Committee for their work in the editing process. We are grateful for the hard work and expertise of all of those who participated.

Brian R. Henry
Chair, 2003–04
Corporate Counseling Committee
Section of Antitrust Law

INTRODUCTION — HOW TO USE *FREQUENTLY ASKED ANTITRUST QUESTIONS*

Frequently Asked Antitrust Questions is a different kind of ABA publication. It is not meant to provide exhaustive answers to complex antitrust questions. It will not provide much help to an antitrust litigator writing an appellate brief.

What *Frequently Asked Antitrust Questions* aims to provide is a quick, jargon-free framework to help answer common antitrust questions that lawyers face every day. For the antitrust lawyer, the publication provides a brief reminder of some antitrust basics plus a list of additional reading materials to help get started and to help ensure that the antitrust lawyer asks the right questions of the client. For the lawyer who does not answer antitrust questions every day, this publication provides quick guidance to help meet client needs.

If you are looking for crisp, clear answers to common antitrust questions, this book will be a valuable resource.

CHAPTER I

COMMUNICATIONS WITH COMPETITORS

A. "We need to know more about our competition — how much protection can we get by calling it 'benchmarking'?"

Merely calling your activities "benchmarking" does not insulate them from possible liability under the antitrust laws. Benchmarking is the process of comparing the business practices of two or more companies in order to improve the business practices of at least the inquiring company. The antitrust risks associated with such efforts do not turn on the label applied, but instead depend upon the type of information gathered, the manner in which it is gathered, from whom it is gathered, and with whom it is shared.

Benchmarking poses little or no risk if the other party is not a competitor or if the information shared is publicly available. A manufacturer of auto parts and a retailer of men's clothing, for example, might profitably benchmark warehousing systems without adversely affecting competition. Similarly, benchmarking through publicly available information should pose little antitrust risk because there is no direct communication among competitors. For example, there should be no antitrust concern in reviewing financial analyst reports that provide an indication of a company's manufacturing costs compared to others in the industry.[1]

---

[1] However, companies should be careful not to engage in indirect communications with competitors through an intermediary such as a financial analyst or a supplier. Such indirect communication plus parallel actions might be viewed as evidence of collusion. *See* Interstate Circuit, Inc. v. United States, 306 U.S. 208, 222 (1939).

The risks associated with benchmarking increase significantly when there is direct contact between competitors. Such contact could result in a determination that an illegal agreement exists between the parties. Section 1 of the Sherman Act prohibits agreements that unreasonably restrain competition.[2] An unlawful agreement may be found even in the absence of a written document or an express verbal understanding between the parties. All that is required is a "unity of purpose or a common design and understanding."[3] An unlawful agreement may be inferred from communications among competitors followed by parallel actions, especially if the competitors would have little motive to take such actions in the absence of a conspiracy. For example, communications between competitors may be used as circumstantial evidence of the formation of a conspiracy when followed by steady or rising prices in the face of falling demand.[4]

Certain business information in certain forms can be exchanged by competitors with little fear of violating the antitrust laws.

---

2 Specifically, Section 1 of the Sherman Act provides that "every contract, combination in the form of trust or otherwise, or conspiracy, in restraint of trade or commerce among the several States, or with foreign nations, is hereby declared to be illegal." 15 U.S.C. § 1. The courts, however, have interpreted this section to apply only to restraints that unreasonably restrain competition. *See* Standard Oil Co. v. United States, 221 U.S. 1, 60–70 (1911).

3 American Tobacco Co. v. United States, 328 U.S. 781, 805 (1946).

4 *See* United States v. Trenton Potteries Co., 273 U.S. 392 (1927); Matsushita Elec. Indus. Co. v. Zenith Radio Corp., 475 U.S. 574 (1986). Todd v. Exxon Corp., 275 F.3d 191 (2d Cir. 2001), illustrates the antitrust perils of competitors exchanging competitively sensitive information. There, oil company employees brought an antitrust action against fourteen major oil companies that together accounted for more than 80 percent of the industry's revenues in the United States. The plaintiffs alleged that the companies violated the Sherman Act by regularly sharing detailed salary data, and that the exchange of such information had the effect of depressing their salaries. The Second Circuit reversed the district court's dismissal of the action, finding that the defendants' data exchange had "anticompetitive potential." *Id.* at 196–97.

Information that is not competitively sensitive may be lawfully exchanged for benchmarking purposes. For example, two competitors might be able to exchange information about the organization of their respective legal departments, so long as they do not exchange salary or other competitively sensitive information or enter into agreements that may unreasonably restrain competition in the relevant labor markets. Competitively sensitive information, such as cost and pricing data, should generally not be exchanged. Nevertheless, information as to past events, including pricing, may be exchanged if sufficiently aggregated so that the recipient cannot discern the pricing (or other information) of individual competitors. Future pricing or other prospective competitive information should never be exchanged. As far back as *Maple Flooring Mfrs. Ass'n. v. United States,*[5] the Supreme Court allowed competitors to exchange information regarding the costs of goods sold, inventory, and pricing, as long as the data were historical and aggregated, and each competitor's information were masked to hide the source of the information.

The Statements of Enforcement Policy and Analytical Principles Relating to Health Care issued in August 1996 by the Federal Trade Commission (FTC) and the Antitrust Division of the Department of Justice (DOJ) provide further helpful guidance concerning information exchanges among competitors.[6] In the *Health Care Statements*, the agencies established an "antitrust safety zone" for exchanges among competitors of price and cost data that are (i) gathered and managed by a third party, (ii) involve data more than three months old, and (iii) involve at least five participants where no individual participant constitutes more than 25 percent of the data on a weighted basis. Moreover, any disseminated information must be sufficiently aggregated to make it impossible to identify the competitively sensitive information relating to any individual participant. Although the *Health Care Statements* apply specifically to the health care industry only, the agencies have made it clear that this safety zone applies generally to other industries as well.

---

5 268 U.S. 563, 582–83 (1924).

6 4 Trade Reg. Rep. (CCH) ¶ 13,153 (Sept. 5, 1996) [hereinafter HEALTH CARE STATEMENTS].

B. "We've been asked to join a trade association — what should we look out for?"

Most trade association activities are procompetitive or at least competitively harmless. Trade associations can disseminate useful knowledge both among members, making them better able to serve their customers, and directly to the customers of members (by cooperative advertising arrangements, for example), making them better able to choose among competing products and services. Moreover, trade associations commonly establish industry standards, which can increase efficiency by making products safer and easier to buy, use, and replace. Trade associations also may disseminate critical historical market information, such as average prices and sales volumes, thereby making markets more transparent and efficient.

Many enforcement actions, however, have arisen from the activities of trade associations or in connection with trade association meetings. This is not surprising, because a trade association is, by definition, a group of competitors. As a consequence, these organizations present opportunities for competitors to engage in activities (even if only unwittingly) that run afoul of the antitrust laws.

There are two general ways in which trade association activity can give rise to antitrust liability; counsel must address both in compliance activities.

(1) Activities of the association itself. The association itself may engage in unlawful conduct. For example, in *American Column & Lumber Co. v. United States*,[7] the Supreme Court ruled that an elaborate agreement implemented by a trade association of lumber companies violated Section 1 of the Sherman Act. The association's so-called "Open Competition Plan" involved association members circulating regular, even daily, reports of their sales, shipments, production, inventory, and prices, as well as estimates of future prices and levels of production. More than fifty years later, in *National Society of*

---

[7] 257 U.S. 377, 409–12 (1921).

Professional Engineers v. United States,[8] the Supreme Court condemned a "Canon of Ethics" adopted by a trade association of professional engineers that prohibited competitive bidding for engineering services. More recently, in 1997 the FTC in *In re International Association of Conference Interpreters*[9] prohibited an association of interpreters from promulgating and enforcing binding fee schedules and work rules. The association activities in all of these cases were condemned because they involved agreements that adversely affected price competition among the members.

By contrast, the DOJ has approved plans by a credit data service for utility companies to share information regarding delinquent account holders to help recover past-due amounts, [10] and by the American Trucking Association to develop and make available to its motor carrier members model contracts that do not include rate provisions and that could be used at the discretion of individual members.[11] The DOJ found no likely anticompetitive harm in these cases because the agreements would not adversely affect price competition among the participants.

Membership limitations or other limitations on participation in trade associations also can raise issues under the antitrust laws. For example, in *Northwest Wholesalers Stationers Inc. v. Pacific Stationery & Printing Co.*, [12] the Supreme Court considered a joint buying cooperative's expulsion of a member. The Court concluded that rule of reason treatment was appropriate because a cooperative needed to be able to "establish and enforce reasonable rules in order to function effectively," and because the plaintiff in that case presented no evidence that the cooperative possessed "market power or exclusive access to an element

---

8 435 U.S. 679, 692 (1978).

9 123 F.T.C. 465, 467 (1997).

10 U.S. Dep't of Justice, Business Review Letter regarding National Consumer Telecommunication Data Exchange (Mar. 12, 2002), *available at* www.usdoj.gov/atr/public/busreview/10825.pdf.

11 U.S. Dep't of Justice, Business Review Letter regarding American Trucking Ass'n (Nov. 15, 2002), *available at* www.usdoj.gov/atr/public/busreview/200481.pdf.

12 472 U.S. 284, 296 (1985).

essential to effective competition."[13] Although the Court held that the existence of procedural safeguards in connection with membership limitations was irrelevant to the analysis, lower courts have continued to use the availability of procedural safeguards as a means of determining the reasonableness of the limitations, as well as the association's intent.[14]

(2) Activities unrelated to legitimate trade association purposes. Trade association meetings often take place in informal environments, and often include social activities. As with any social situation, the participants may be tempted to try to promote trust and friendship among their peers by sharing confidences "off the record." They may feel tempted to commiserate over low industry prices or a particularly difficult customer or competitor, or share information regarding an upcoming strategic initiative. Unfortunately, even innocent statements about such topics can be used later as evidence of an agreement to fix prices, allocate customers or markets, or jointly refuse to deal with other market participants.

Moreover, unscrupulous businesspeople can use trade association events as a cover for unlawful cartel activities. Indeed, many of the most recent DOJ international cartel cases involve conspiratorial activities conducted at or under the guise of trade association meetings.[15]

In order to ensure that the activities of a trade association do not pose antitrust risks, the trade association should have procedural safeguards firmly in place. Counsel for individual members of the organization should confirm that appropriate safeguards are in place *before* approving

---

[13] *Id.*; *see also* Massachusetts School of Law v. Am. Bar Ass'n, 107 F.3d 1026, 1035 (3d Cir. 1997) (refusal to invite nonmember school to annual conference not a boycott because conference was not essential facility for recruiting students).

[14] *See, e.g.,* Pretz v. Holstein Friesian Ass'n, 698 F. Supp. 1531, 1540 (D. Kan. 1988) (considering procedural safeguards); *but see* Martin v. Am. Kennel Club, Inc., 697 F. Supp. 997, 999 n.4 (N.D. Ill. 1988) (refusing to consider procedural safeguards).

[15] *See, e.g.*, United States v. Eisai Co., Criminal No. 399-CR-355 (C.D. Tex. Sept. 9, 1999), *available at* www.usdoj.gov/atr/cases/13600/3664.htm.

employee or client participation. Appropriate procedural safeguards include:

- **Policies.** As in any compliance area, protection against liability begins with making certain that all who are involved have a clear understanding of the rules. The association should therefore have clearly stated and widely disseminated written antitrust policies. Often, a trade association will read or distribute its antitrust compliance policy at the start of every meeting.

- **Meetings.** It is important that procedures be established and meticulously followed to ensure that meetings are conducted in a manner that minimizes the risk of unlawful conduct. These procedures should include:
  - ➢ The establishment of an agenda that is distributed and reviewed by association counsel well in advance of meetings.
  - ➢ The giving of an antitrust "warning" at the beginning of every meeting advising participants that compliance with the antitrust laws is mandatory.
  - ➢ Where appropriate, attendance by counsel conversant in the antitrust laws.
  - ➢ The taking of accurate minutes, which should be reviewed by association counsel before they are distributed.[16]

- **Information Sharing.** As stated in the previous section, the exchange of price information among competitors presents a particularly significant risk of liability under Section 1. Information sharing can be evidence of a price-fixing agreement when the reason for the exchange appears to be to monitor and enforce an agreement on prices. Information exchanges also

---

[16] For additional considerations, see David A. Bagwell, *Corporate Activity in Trade Associations and Standard Setting: Your Momma's Rules* (Apr. 7, 2000), *available at* www.abanet.org/antitrust/committees/trade assoc/yourmomma.pdf.

may result in antitrust liability even in the absence of evidence of an intention to affect prices. Such information exchanges will be evaluated after the fact by investigators or a jury who might be skeptical of the proffered business justification for the exchange. To minimize this risk, information sharing in a trade association context should be consistent with the principles discussed at pages 1–3 above.

Counsel also should ensure that the conduct of clients at trade association meetings does not give rise to liability. Company counsel initially should approve participation in any new association. Once that process is completed, company counsel should identify the particular employees who will be involved in trade association activities and ensure that those employees receive adequate antitrust training. Employees attending trade association meetings should, at a minimum, be instructed that:

- There is no exemption from the antitrust laws for trade association activity. Any conduct that would be unlawful outside the context of an association is just as unlawful when an association is involved.
- The rules regarding appropriate trade association conduct apply at social gatherings as well as at scheduled official meetings or events. Any statement, whether made in a formal or an informal context, has the potential to become evidence in the courtroom. Prices can be fixed just as easily on the golf course Saturday as on the telephone Monday.
- The discussion at meetings should be limited to the topics on the agenda that has been preapproved by counsel.
- "Rump" sessions should be avoided. Any subcommittees, workgroups, and the like should have clearly defined tasks.
- If anticompetitive behavior occurs at a meeting, protest publicly. If the conduct does not cease, leave the meeting *conspicuously,* and ask the secretary of the meeting to make a note that you have done so. In addition, any inappropriate conduct should be reported immediately to counsel.

Counsel must impress upon every employee involved in trade association activities that this is an area in which both appearance and substance are important. The simple fact that a meeting between competitors took place, or that a flippant remark was made that did not reflect the true intentions of the participants or the reality of their interactions with one another, can take on a sinister appearance in the context of a subsequent investigation or litigation.

The issues discussed above apply any time competitors gather at the same location or on a telephone or videoconference. For example, competitors often attend meetings or social events sponsored by suppliers, or meet at trade shows. Company counsel should therefore ensure that employees who attend any event where competitors are present receive antitrust training in accordance with the principles outlined above.

C. "Our trade association is working on some industry standards — can we participate?"

The promulgation of standards can be an important, procompetitive function of a trade association. The benefits of developing industry standards are widely recognized. For example, standards help to ensure that products from different firms are compatible, thus allowing consumers to enjoy the benefits of rivalry among competitors. Because standards make it easier for firms to design compatible products, they are often particularly important in the initial stages of the introduction of a new technology. An industry standard, such as industry safety certifications, also may provide important information to consumers.

Counsel should confirm that standard-setting decisions affecting competitors are made in a way that is procedurally transparent. In *Allied Tube & Conduit Corp. v. Indian Head, Inc.*,[17] the Supreme Court held that standards promulgated by competitors are lawful if "based on the merits of objective expert judgments through procedures that prevent

---

[17] 486 U.S. 492 (1988).

the standard-setting process from being biased by members with economic interests in stifling competition."[18] There, producers of steel conduit packed a trade association meeting with supporters in order to defeat an amendment to the association's model fire code that would have approved the use of plastic conduit, an alternative to steel conduit. The Court found that, because many jurisdictions adopted the model fire code, the ballot-stuffing by the steel conduit manufacturers unreasonably excluded plastic conduit manufacturers from the market.

In antitrust challenges to standard-setting, courts generally focus on whether there has been an abuse of the process, as was the case in *Allied Tube*, rather than on the merits of the standards at issue. The key, therefore, is to ensure that safeguards are in place to prevent procedural abuses of the process that have the effect of excluding rivals whether through ballot-stuffing tactics as in *Allied Tube*, or through other tactics that have the effect of excluding interested parties, such as manipulation of the membership selection process.[19]

In addition, an association's standards may run afoul of the antitrust laws if they are not reasonably related to their stated procompetitive purpose. For example, in its challenge to the accreditation activities of the American Bar Association (ABA), the DOJ attacked a standard that required law schools to pay faculty compensation that was "comparable" to law schools in their "peer group."[20] The government alleged that the standards were designed to increase faculty salaries and improve working conditions rather than to serve their stated purpose of providing useful information to state bar officials and prospective law students regarding the quality of law schools in the United States. This enforcement action was resolved by a consent decree that, among other things, prohibits the ABA from

---

18 *Id.* at 501.

19 *See* Jennifer L. Gray, *Antitrust Guidelines for Participating in Standard Setting Efforts,* CORPORATE COUNSELING REPORT 22 (Spring 2001), *available at* www.abanet.org/antitrust/mo/premium-at/cc/spring2001.pdf.

20 United States v. Am. Bar Ass'n, Civil Action No. 95-1211 (CR) (D.D.C., filed June 27, 1995), *available at* www.usdoj.gov/atr/cases/f4500/4571.htm.

conditioning the accreditation of a law school on the salaries, fringe benefits or other compensation paid to its faculty or administrators.

Counsel should ensure that employees who participate in standards organizations understand their disclosure obligations and disclose required information accurately. In *Dell Computer*, the FTC charged Dell with violating Section 5 of the Federal Trade Commission Act in connection with Dell's attempt to enforce patent rights against users of a standard that allegedly infringed those rights. The FTC charged that Dell had expressly certified to a standard-setting body that it possessed no patents that would be infringed by the standard. Dell thereafter sought to enforce its patent rights against users of the standard. In March of 1996, the FTC approved a Consent Order under which Dell agreed not to enforce its patent rights against any company using the standard and agreed not to engage in similar conduct with respect to future standard-setting activity.[21]

Although *Dell* does not establish an absolute duty to disclose the existence of intellectual property rights that might relate to a standard, employees who participate in standard-setting organizations should understand that false or uninformed representations may create liability for the company and may even prevent the company from exploiting its patents or other intellectual property related to that standard.[22]

---

21 Dell Computer Corp., 121 F.T.C. 616 (1996). *See also* Federal Trade Comm'n Press Release, FTC Charges Unocal with Anticompetitive Conduct Related to Reformulated Gasoline (Mar. 4, 2003) (announcing FTC complaint alleging that Unocal gained monopoly power by misrepresenting to California Air Resources Board and industry groups proprietary nature of low emission gasoline formulation), *available at* www.ftc.gov/opa/2003/03/unocal.htm; Federal Trade Comm'n Press Release, FTC Issues Complaint Against Rambus, Inc. (June 19, 2002) (announcing FTC complaint alleging scheme to deceive industry standard setting organization), *available at* www.ftc.gov/opa/2002/06/rambus.htm; *but see* Federal Trade Comm'n Press Release, Administrative Law Judge Dismisses Complaint Against Unocal for Alleged Anticompetitive Practices Related to Carb Gasoline (Nov. 26, 2003), *available at* www.ftc.gov/opa/2003/11/unionoil.htm.

22 *See* Rambus Inc. v. Infineon Tech. AG, 318 F.3d 1081 (Fed. Cir. 2003).

Employees must use caution in making any representations to standard-setting groups. It may be advisable to provide any relevant statements in writing so that the representation can be reviewed by intellectual property experts within the company as well as by legal counsel.

D. "Where can I go for more information?"

A. "We need to know more about our competition — how much protection can we get by calling it 'benchmarking'?"

- ABA SECTION OF ANTITRUST LAW, ANTITRUST LAW DEVELOPMENTS 98 (5th ed. 2002) [hereinafter ANTITRUST LAW DEVELOPMENTS (FIFTH)].
- ABA SECTION OF ANTITRUST LAW, A PRIMER ON THE LAW OF INFORMATION EXCHANGE (2d ed. 2002).
- Roxann E. Henry, *Could an Information Exchange Trigger a $100 Million Fine?*, 14 ANTITRUST 1 (Summer 2000).
- Brian L. Henry, *Benchmarking and Antitrust*, 62 ANTITRUST L.J. 483 (1994).

B. "We've been asked to join a trade association — what should we look out for?"

- ANTITRUST LAW DEVELOPMENTS (FIFTH) at 114–18.
- ABA SECTION OF ANTITRUST LAW, TRADE AND PROFESSIONAL ASSOCIATIONS: AVOIDING THE ANTITRUST MINEFIELD (1994).

C. "Our trade association is working on some industry standards — can we participate?"

- ANTITRUST LAW DEVELOPMENTS (FIFTH) at 114–18, 1227–28.
- David J. Teece and Edward F. Sherry, *Standards Setting and Antitrust*, 87 MINN. L. REV. 1931 (June 2003).
- Alden F. Abbott and Theodore A. Gebhard, *Standard-Setting Disclosure Policies: Evaluating Antitrust Policies in Light of* Rambus, 16 ANTITRUST 29 (Summer 2002).
- Joseph Kattan, *Antitrust Implications: Disclosures and Commitments to Standard-Setting Organizations,* 16 ANTITRUST 22 (Summer 2002).

- U.S. DEP'T OF JUSTICE AND FEDERAL TRADE COMM'N, ANTITRUST GUIDELINES FOR COLLABORATIONS AMONG COMPETITORS (2000), *reprinted in* 4 Trade Reg. Rep. (CCH) ¶ 13,161.

CHAPTER II

MERGERS AND JOINT VENTURES

A. "We are contemplating merging with or acquiring another company — what sort of antitrust approvals will we need?"

A merger or acquisition raises both procedural and substantive antitrust questions. Each set of questions is discussed separately below.

The procedural question is whether a filing must be made to any government agency prior to closing the transaction. In the United States, the mandatory preacquisition notification system is commonly referred to as Hart-Scott-Rodino, or "HSR," after the antitrust statute that, among other things, established premerger filing requirements in the United States for certain large transactions.[1]

The HSR process is intended to provide the FTC and the DOJ with (i) notice of transactions that may raise antitrust concerns, (ii) an "initial waiting period" during which to consider the competitive aspects of a proposed transaction and decide whether to take action to block the proposed transaction, and (iii) the statutory power to require the parties to provide basic information about a proposed transaction and its participants (and, at the agencies' request, to obtain more-extensive information from the parties or other industry participants to facilitate

[1] Hart-Scott-Rodino Antitrust Improvements Act of 1976, Pub. L. No. 94-435, § 201, 90 Stat. 1390 (codified as amended at 15 U.S.C. § 18a). The regulations adopted by the FTC to implement HSR appear at 16 C.F.R. §§ 801–803. The FTC is charged with administering the HSR premerger notification process, although filings are made to both the FTC and the DOJ, and both agencies are responsible for substantive reviews of proposed transactions (although in any particular case only one of the agencies conducts the investigation).

their review of the proposed transaction). During the initial waiting period following a transaction's notification to the FTC and DOJ under HSR, and any extensions to the initial waiting period, the parties are not permitted to close the proposed transaction. For most acquisitions (other than cash tender offers and acquisitions subject to bankruptcy approval) the initial waiting period is thirty days; for these other categories of transactions, the waiting period is fifteen days.

If the FTC and the DOJ take no action with respect to the proposed acquisition within the initial waiting period, the parties are deemed to have received clearance under HSR and may proceed with the closing of their deal. However, either the FTC or the DOJ may extend the waiting period by formally requesting information regarding the proposed transaction (commonly called a "Second Request"). Second Requests are often quite comprehensive, involving extensive requests for documents, written questions, and even interviews or sworn testimony.[2] Once the parties have substantially complied with the Second Request, another thirty-day waiting period (fifteen in the case of cash tender offers and acquisitions subject to bankruptcy court approval) must be observed before the parties can close the transaction.

When is a filing under HSR required? HSR generally requires a filing if two threshold tests are met: (i) the size of person test and (ii) the size of transaction test.[3]

The size of the person threshold is passed if the "ultimate parent entity" (the entity not controlled by any other entity plus all the entities the ultimate parent entity controls)[4] of either the acquiring or acquired persons has annual net sales or total assets of $100 million or more and

---

2 The agencies have made available a "model" Second Request that provides a good indication of the types of information commonly requested. *See Model Second Request*, *available at* www.ftc.gov/bc/modelguide.htm.

3 A third threshold requirement requires that one of the parties to the transaction be engaged in interstate commerce. This requirement is met in nearly every case that is not otherwise exempt.

4 The HSR regulations provide complete definitions of "person," "ultimate parent entity," and "control." *See* 16 C.F.R. § 801.1(a)(1), (a)(3), and (b).

the ultimate parent entity of the other person has annual net sales or total assets of $10 million or more. Counsel must consult the most recent regularly prepared balance sheet and the most recent annual statement of income and expense for the necessary data.[5] For transactions valued at greater than $200 million, the size of person test is ignored and, absent an exemption, a filing must be made.[6]

The second threshold, the size of the transaction test, is passed if, as a result of the transaction, the acquiring person would hold voting securities and/or assets of the acquired person with a value greater than $50 million.[7] The filing thresholds will be adjusted for changes in Gross Domestic Product beginning in the U.S. government's 2005 fiscal year.

Application of these thresholds can depend on the corporate structures involved. The thresholds described above apply to most stock or asset transactions between two or more corporations. Formations of corporate joint ventures, however, are treated slightly differently. For instance, each of the parties forming the venture is considered an "acquiring person."[8] Formation of partnerships and the acquisition of partnership interests generally are not reportable, because partnership interests are not considered "voting securities." The acquisition of 100 percent of a partnership, however, is considered an acquisition of the partnership's assets and could be reportable under HSR.[9] The formation of limited liability companies (LLCs) requires an HSR filing if, as a result of the transaction, two or more pre-existing, separately controlled businesses will be contributed to the LLC, and at least one of the members will control the LLC. Acquisitions of existing LLC

---

5 For further explanation of such measurements, *see* 16 C.F.R. § 801.11(c)(1) and (2).

6 *See* 15 U.S.C. § 18a(a)(2)(A).

7 *See* 15 U.S.C. § 18a(a)(3). Counsel also must consult the regulations if there is a question whether the securities that are to be acquired are "voting securities" for HSR purposes. The term "assets" is not defined under HSR, but can include licenses under certain circumstances.

8 *See* 16 C.F.R. § 801.40 (complete explanation and thresholds).

9 *See* ABA SECTION OF ANTITRUST LAW, PREMERGER NOTIFICATION PRACTICE MANUAL, Interp. No. 93 (3d ed. 2003) [hereinafter PREMERGER NOTIFICATION PRACTICE MANUAL].

membership interests will only be reportable if the acquiring person will hold 100 percent of the interests of an LLC, or the acquiring person contributes a business to the LLC in exchange for its LLC membership interests.[10]

Even if all the thresholds are met, one of the many exemptions to the filing requirements might make it unnecessary to make an HSR filing. For instance, acquisitions of goods and realty made "in the ordinary course of business" are exempt.[11] Other exemptions include certain intraperson transactions, certain acquisitions of voting securities made "solely for the purpose of investment," and certain transactions involving foreign persons, assets, or voting securities.[12] Acquisitions of real estate also are generally exempt from HSR filing requirements.

There are several useful sources for further guidance regarding HSR. It should be noted that the HSR process involves a highly technical set of statutory and regulatory law, and the final result can be determined by any one of a number of formal or informal interpretations. Moreover, HSR notification analyses are very fact specific, and the applicable regulations and interpretations can change over time. Counsel should be sure to read the law and accompanying regulations carefully, and to consult one of the sources mentioned below for further guidance as appropriate. A particularly helpful resource is a monograph published by the ABA Section of Antitrust Law that provides a thorough review of the entire merger review process.[13] Also very useful is the *Premerger Notification Practice Manual*, which is a collection and discussion of FTC staff informal interpretations relating to HSR.[14] In addition, the

---

10 *See* 64 Fed. Reg. 5808 (Feb. 5, 1999) for a complete explanation of the FTC's interpretation of the regulations regarding LLCs.

11 15 U.S.C. § 18a(c)(1); 16 C.F.R. § 802.1.

12 All of the exemptions in the HSR regulations are contained in 16 C.F.R. § 802.

13 ABA SECTION OF ANTITRUST LAW, THE MERGER REVIEW PROCESS: A STEP-BY-STEP GUIDE TO FEDERAL MERGER REVIEW (2001).

14 PREMERGER NOTIFICATION PRACTICE MANUAL, *supra* note 9.

FTC Web site contains a wealth of HSR information.[15] Moreover, the staff of the FTC Premerger Notification Office is available to provide informal guidance over the telephone, on a confidential basis, on particularly difficult, as well as routine, questions.[16]

The HSR form requires extensive company information. If a filing is required, usually both the acquired and acquiring persons must file a notification form and submit documents that describe the parties and the transaction, even if the transaction in question is not a negotiated one (for example, the target company of a hostile tender offer may be required to file).

Certain sections of the form require basic information concerning the filing party, such as its name and address and the name of a contact person. Other sections require more detailed information. Item 5 of the form, for example, requires revenue information for products and services sold during the most recent year and an earlier base year.[17] Parties must use the product codes of the North American Industrial Classification System (NAICS) established by the Bureau of the Census. Item 6 of the form requires information about subsidiaries and large shareholders of the entity filing the notification, and certain voting securities held by the entity. Information regarding Items 5 and 6 can be collected even in the absence of any proposed transaction, so that responses are ready and available should it become necessary to make an HSR filing.

Other parts of the HSR form require information particular to the transaction. Item 3(a) requires a general description of the transaction, including names and addresses of all parties, a description of the

---

15 The Web site address is www.ftc.gov/bc/hsr.htm.

16 The current phone number for the FTC Premerger Notification Office is 202-326-3100. The FTC staff does not issue informal opinions in writing. Counsel may, however, confirm by letter the informal advice given by staff. Formal interpretations are available, but the process is usually too time-consuming to be helpful in a particular transaction.

17 The Federal Trade Commission adjusts the base year in conjunction with certain adjustments by the Census Bureau. Generally, the base years are those ending in "2" or "7."

consideration involved, and the expected date of consummation. Items 3(b) and (c) require additional information concerning the assets or voting securities to be acquired. Item 7 requires the listing of NAICS codes that apply to both of the filing parties. Item 8 requires the acquiring person to provide certain information regarding any previous acquisitions involving any of the NAICS codes listed in Item 7.

An affidavit from an officer of each party that his or her company intends in good faith to complete the transaction usually must accompany the form. In addition, an officer or director must certify under oath that the information provided in the notification form is true and correct.[18]

Finally, the form must be accompanied by certain documents that further describe the parties and the transaction. Item 3(d) requires the submission of a copy of the executed agreement or letter of intent. Items 4(a) and (b) require submission of certain documents routinely filed with the United States Securities and Exchange Commission. Finally, Item 4(c) requires submission of "all studies, surveys, analyses, and reports prepared by or for any officer(s) or director(s) for purposes of evaluating or analyzing the acquisition." Item 4(c) documents receive close attention during the initial investigation because they are likely to reveal the parties' views of the competitive impact of the transaction.

Counsel should ensure that a thorough search is conducted of the files of company personnel who are likely to have in their possession 4(c) documents. The agencies may react harshly if they believe that the parties have not been diligent in searching for and producing 4(c) documents. In *United States v. Blackstone Capital Partners II Merchant Banking Fund L.P.*,[19] the DOJ charged a merchant bank and the general partner who signed the bank's HSR certification with violating the HSR Act by failing to submit several 4(c) documents, including a memorandum that would have allowed the agencies to evaluate the transaction's competitive effects. The bank agreed to pay a penalty of almost $3 million and, for the first time, HSR penalties (in this instance

---

18 The certification can be made by a general partner in the case of a partnership or a person exercising similar functions in other organizations. *See* 16 C.F.R. § 803.6.

19 Civ. No. 1:99CV00795 (D.D.C. Mar. 30, 1999), *available at* www.usdoj.gov/atr/cases/f9200/9291.pdf.

$50,000) were imposed upon the individual who signed the certification. The government charged that the general partner, as the author of the omitted memorandum, knew or should have known that the HSR certification was inaccurate. Similarly in *United States* v. *The Hearst Trust*,[20] the FTC imposed a civil penalty of $4 million as a result of a December 1997 HSR filing that failed to include all 4(c) documents and also failed to include a list of such documents withheld on a claim of privilege as required by the HSR regulations.

It should be noted that the contents of notification forms and the documents submitted with them are kept confidential by the FTC and the DOJ and are exempt from disclosure to private parties and other government agencies. Even the fact that a filing has been made is kept confidential. It is generally not possible to learn whether a filing has been made or whether a waiting period has been terminated with respect to a particular transaction. However, if early termination is sought and granted, the grant of early termination will be made public by the FTC.

A fee, the size of which is determined by the size of the transaction, must accompany the form. The buyer is responsible for paying the fee to the FTC, although the parties may choose to allocate it otherwise by private agreement. The current fee is $45,000 for transactions valued at less than $100 million, $125,000 for transactions valued between $100 million and $500 million, and $280,000 for transactions valued at $500 million or more.

As discussed above, once all the filings and fees are received by the FTC and DOJ, the agencies usually have thirty days (fifteen days in the case of a cash tender offer or a sale in bankruptcy) to make an initial determination of any adverse competitive effects of the transaction. First, the two agencies decide which of them, if either, will investigate the transaction. This "clearance" process is usually completed within two weeks. The agency with the greater experience or expertise with the industries or parties involved in the transaction usually will receive clearance from the other to investigate the transaction. That agency then uses some or all of the remaining time in the initial waiting period to

---

[20] Civ. No. 1:01CV02119 (D.D.C. Oct. 11, 2001), *available at* www.ftc.gov/opa/2001/10/hearst.htm.

gather information about the potential competitive effects of the transaction. The information usually is gathered informally from public sources, the parties, their customers and competitors, and any other knowledgeable sources. At any time during the initial waiting period, the agency can end the investigation and grant "early termination" of the waiting period.[21]

At the conclusion of the waiting period, the agencies (i) can allow the transaction to proceed by taking no further action, or (ii) can extend the initial waiting period through the issuance of a Second Request. A Second Request usually indicates that the agency has competitive concerns about the transaction.

Where the regulators identify a competitive issue with respect to a proposed transaction, it is common for them to negotiate voluntary settlements with the parties. Voluntary settlements generally require the parties to divest all or a portion of either the acquired or acquiring person's business in the market in which competitive issues are deemed to arise. Such divestitures are required to be made within strict time limits and subject to the terms of formal consent orders approved by the FTC (with respect to investigations conducted by the FTC) or a U.S. District Court (with respect to investigations conducted by the DOJ).

Failure to comply with HSR filing requirements may lead to the imposition of civil penalties of up to $11,000 per day payable by the company and each of its officers or directors who failed to comply.[22]

At least sixty-five countries have established their own premerger notification requirements that may differ significantly from the HSR process. A relatively small amount of sales or assets in a foreign country may trigger a filing obligation and payment of a filing fee there. Counsel for firms with foreign sales or assets involved in a transaction should therefore be familiar with the filing thresholds of each

---

21 The parties must check the box on the form to request early termination. Early terminations are published in the Federal Register and on the FTC's Web site. Early terminations granted during the preceding week are also available by calling the FTC's recorded information line at 202-326-2222.

22 15 U.S.C. § 18a(g)(1).

country in which the company has sales or assets.[23] Some foreign notifications are voluntary. Under the notification regimes of other countries, such as Brazil, notification may be mandatory but the parties may consummate their transaction prior to obtaining approval from the antitrust authorities.

Although no state has enacted a premerger notification statute, individual states are able to subpoena documents pursuant to their state antitrust statutes prior to the closing of a transaction. In addition, the states, under the auspices of the National Association of Attorneys General, have established a Premerger Compact facilitating cooperation among multiple states investigating a particular transaction. Counsel should be aware that states and the federal agencies have increasingly cooperated on merger investigations. Moreover, one or more states may independently investigate and challenge a transaction, even if the FTC and the DOJ do not.

The answer to the procedural question (file or not?) does not, of course, answer the substantive question: Will this transaction adversely affect competition in appropriately defined markets?[24] The competitive effects of mergers and acquisitions are evaluated primarily under Section 7 of the Clayton Act, which prohibits such transactions where "the effect of such acquisition may be substantially to lessen competition, or tend to create a monopoly."[25]

---

23 The Web site of the International Competition Network includes links to foreign merger control laws at www.internationalcompetition network.org/mergerscountries.html. *See also* Michael J. Cicero, *International Merger Control,* 15 ANTITRUST 15, 16-17 (Spring 2001).

24 The process used by the federal agencies to consider whether a proposed transaction violates Section 7 is detailed in the 1992 *Horizontal Merger Guidelines*, issued jointly by the DOJ and the FTC and amended in 1997. U.S. DEP'T OF JUSTICE & FEDERAL TRADE COMM'N 1992 HORIZONTAL MERGER GUIDELINES, *reprinted in* 4 Trade Reg. Rep. (CCH) ¶ 13,104 (Apr. 17, 1997) [hereinafter MERGER GUIDELINES].

25 15 U.S.C § 18. Section 7 of the Clayton Act applies to *all* mergers and acquisitions, not only those notifiable under HSR. Consequently, the

The substantive analysis should be undertaken when the proposed transaction is first seriously considered. Generally, the first step of the analysis is to define both a product and geographic market. Market definition is often the determining factor in merger cases. In general, the agencies (and eventually the courts) attempt to determine the other products and geographic areas that consumers could turn to if the merged firms instituted a small but significant nontransitory increase in price. Once the product and geographic markets are determined, the market participants are identified. For example, market participants could be other producers of the product that compete with the merging parties, plus companies that produce the product for internal consumption, and those who are "potential competitors" of the merging parties.[26] Market shares are then determined for these participants followed by a determination of market concentration. The concentration measure can then be compared to some standard and, at least preliminarily, help answer the substantive question.

The review of a court or agency starts, but does not end, with market concentration. Traditional merger analysis in the United States focuses on, among other things, two questions: (i) whether the merger would create or enhance the competitive strength of the parties to such an extent that it gives them unilateral power over price or other aspects of competition; and/or (ii) whether the merger would significantly increase the likelihood of sustainable collusion. The first question depends, in part, on the market share of the merged firm. If that share remains low following the combination—or even if it is large but there are other firms of nearly equal size—there is a presumption that the merged firm would not be able to engage unilaterally in anticompetitive behavior.

DOJ and the FTC have the authority to, and do, investigate and challenge transactions that are not reportable under HSR.

26 The *Merger Guidelines* differentiate between "uncommitted entrants" and "committed entrants" based on whether certain costs must be expended in order to enter the market. The *Merger Guidelines* count these entrants as participants if it is determined that they would enter quickly under certain conditions. *Id.*

Conversely, if the merged firm's market share following the combination is high, this would be seen as evidence of the postmerger firm's market power. The second question depends, again in part, on the number and size distribution of the firms in the relevant market.

The most widely accepted measure of market concentration is the Herfindahl-Hirschman Index (HHI) of market concentration. HHIs are computed by summing the squares of the individual market shares of all market participants. The *Merger Guidelines* divide the spectrum of market concentration into three categories: unconcentrated (a postmerger HHI below 1000), moderately concentrated (a postmerger HHI between 1000 and 1800), and concentrated (a postmerger HHI above 1800). The *Merger Guidelines* assess the competitive effects of a transaction by comparing premerger HHIs with postmerger HHIs as follows:

Unconcentrated Postmerger HHI. Mergers resulting in unconcentrated markets are deemed unlikely to have adverse competitive effects and ordinarily require no further analysis no matter how significant the difference between the premerger and postmerger HHIs.

Moderately Concentrated Postmerger HHI. Mergers producing an increase in the HHI of less than 100 points in moderately concentrated postmerger markets are deemed unlikely to have adverse competitive consequences and ordinarily require no further analysis. Mergers producing an increase in the HHI of more than 100 points in moderately concentrated postmerger markets potentially raise significant competitive concerns depending on the factors set forth in other sections of the *Merger Guidelines*.

Concentrated Postmerger HHI. Mergers producing an increase in the HHI of less than 50 points, even in highly concentrated postmerger markets, are considered unlikely to have adverse competitive consequences and ordinarily require no further analysis. Mergers producing an increase in the HHI of more than 50 points in highly concentrated postmerger markets potentially raise significant competitive concerns, depending on the factors set forth in other sections of the

Merger Guidelines. Where the postmerger HHI exceeds 1800, it will be presumed that mergers producing an increase in the HHI of more than 100 points are likely to create or enhance market power or to facilitate its exercise. The presumption may be overcome by a showing that factors set forth in other sections of the *Merger Guidelines* make it unlikely that the merger will have such effects.

In addition to HHI measures, the *Merger Guidelines* refer to other factors as well that are relevant to the competitive analysis. The other factors referred to in the *Merger Guidelines* include the structure of the industry (that is, the degree of industry concentration, product homogeneity, the degree of industry pricing transparency, fungibility of product offerings, the existence of countervailing customer power, and capacity levels), the likelihood and ease of new market entry, and the level of potential efficiencies resulting from a proposed transaction.

Arguably the most important of these additional factors is the ease of new entry. Generally, if it is easy for new firms to effectively enter the market in a timely manner, and such entry is likely, the current market participants will be unable to exercise market power. Conditions that could prevent easy entry include long lead times, large capital expenditures, and the unavailability of necessary technical knowledge.

The type of products involved in the proposed transaction also can be important. If the products of the merging parties are generally unlikely to be differentiated (as in, say, a market for wheat), then coordination among the remaining competitors will be easier. If the products of the merging parties are differentiated, the agencies will examine whether the products of the merging parties are "close substitutes." Products may be close substitutes when many customers have a strong preference for the products of the merging parties over those of other competitors.[27]

---

[27] F.T.C. v. Staples, Inc., 970 F. Supp. 1066 (D.D.C. 1997), is a case where the "product" involved included the method of distribution. While there were many sellers of consumable office products, the merging parties (Office Depot and Staples) were one of a small number of participants that sold them through a superstore format.

Another factor that the parties often want the agencies and courts to consider is the expected efficiencies from the transaction. The agencies recognize that some mergers may create significant efficiencies, such as lower prices, improved quality of the products produced by the merging parties, enhanced service, or new products. The purported efficiencies must be merger specific (that is, unlikely to be accomplished in the absence of the merger). The greater the potential adverse competitive effects of a proposed merger, the greater must be the efficiencies to overcome these concerns. As a consequence, arguable efficiencies will rarely save from antitrust attack a clearly anticompetitive merger, such as one that would result in the merged firm possessing a monopoly in a relevant market.

Finally, in rare circumstances, an otherwise anticompetitive merger will be allowed to proceed if the seller is a "failing firm," the buyer is the only possible buyer, and reorganization of the "failing firm" under the bankruptcy code is not possible.

The analysis of vertical mergers usually focuses on potential foreclosure or facilitation of collusion in one of the markets. When a supplier and a customer merge, competitors of the supplier might be "foreclosed" from a key outlet for their products. Similarly, competitors of the customer might be "foreclosed" from a key input to their products. This analysis requires an evaluation of both the "upstream" and "downstream" markets. If there are many participants in both markets, the possibility of foreclosure is low. Vertical mergers also might facilitate horizontal collusion. One theory pursued by the agencies suggests that an upstream supplier might be able to learn proprietary information about its competitors by merging with a customer that buys from several suppliers.[28] Many antitrust concerns in vertical transactions can be alleviated through structural changes or behavioral restrictions.

---

[28] *See, e.g.*, TRW, Inc., No. 981-0081, 63 Fed. Reg. 1866 (F.T.C. Jan. 12, 1998) (aid to public comment), 125 F.T.C. 496 (1998) (decision and order); United States v. Lockheed Martin Corp., Civ. No. 1:98CV00731 (D.D.C. Mar. 23, 1998) (verified complaint), *available at* www.usdoj.gov/atr/cases/f2200/2237.htm.

State and foreign antitrust authorities will start with a similar analysis but might consider other factors. The states have issued their own set of merger guidelines through the National Association of Attorneys General (NAAG).[29] International antitrust authorities also frequently approach merger review from a different perspective. For example, European Union law looks at whether the proposed transaction will "create or strengthen a dominant position as a result of which effective competition would be significantly impeded in all or a substantial portion of the European Union," which is similar but not identical to the United States' "substantial lessening of competition" standard. Even when the analysis is identical, the effects of the transaction might vary in the different jurisdictions and, consequently, the final determination might be different. Similarly, the effects in the varying jurisdictions might appear to be the same, but different authorities, with different enforcement priorities, might reach different conclusions as to whether approval should be granted.

B. "We're going forward with a merger or acquisition — what can we talk about during due diligence?"

Clients sometimes imagine that there exists a safe harbor from antitrust liability for due diligence activities. There are several reasons why, when a firm is negotiating to purchase a competing firm or business, the negotiators may not recognize the risks posed by the discussions themselves.

- First, there is the situation familiar to lawyers in almost any business situation: because the parties are pursuing an agreement, they naturally resist contemplating what will happen if they fail and the deal falls through.
- Second, they may be dealing with a company with which they have competed in the past, and consequently there may even be hard feelings to overcome if the deal is to take place. Because

---

[29] The NAAG *Horizontal Merger Guidelines*, *reprinted in* 4 Trade Reg. Rep. (CCH) ¶¶ 13,405, 13,406 (Apr. 13, 1993).

part of their objective is to build a relationship of trust, they may resist efforts to set limits on what can and cannot be discussed.

- Finally, in a situation in which the seller may be dealing with several potential buyers at once, it is easy for the businesspeople to forget that liability does not depend on reaching a final agreement to consummate the transaction.

The corporate counselor must at the outset minimize risks arising from the negotiation of a merger or acquisition and due diligence activities.[30] The exchange of competitively sensitive information, such as customer-specific current and future pricing and market data during the due diligence period may raise issues under the antitrust laws if the prospective transaction parties are competitors. The antitrust concern is that the disclosure of sensitive information may harm competition between the buyer and seller before closing or later, if the parties decide not to proceed with the deal or the transaction does not close for some other reason (including because the antitrust regulators block it).

The FTC and the DOJ have focused on preconsummation exchanges of sensitive information among purchasers and sellers. In *Insilco Corp.*,[31] a challenge to an acquisition involving two of the major aluminum tube manufacturers in the United States, the FTC alleged that, prior to the closing of the transaction, the companies exchanged customer-specific price information, price formulas, and current and future pricing plans and strategies. The government contended that, because the markets at issue were highly concentrated, the data exchange had the potential to injure competition. The FTC brought an enforcement action challenging this preclosing information exchange even though the transaction ultimately was consummated. The FTC and

---

30 *See* William Blumenthal, *The Scope of Permissible Coordination Between Merging Entities Prior to Consummation*, 63 ANTITRUST L.J. 1 (1994); Ilene Knable Gotts & Michael B. Miller, *Information Sharing and Joint Activities in the Pre-Consummation Context: How to Plan for the Post-Transaction Entity*, ANTITRUST REPORT 2 (March 1999).

31 File No. 961 0106, Docket No. C-3783 (Jan. 30, 1998), *available at* www.ftc.gov/os/caselist/c3783.htm.

the parties entered into a consent agreement that prohibited the parties from sharing certain sensitive information in future transactions, including information regarding customer-specific price and cost data, current or future pricing plans, or current or future strategies or policies relating to competition.

Counsel can minimize the risks by advising against the exchange of certain types of information. One useful rule of thumb that some counsel ask is, "Is this the type of information that competitors never share absent a prospective deal?" If the answer is yes, then it might be necessary to limit the exchange or reduce the commercial sensitivity of the information by, for example, (i) limiting the data to historical information only, (ii) aggregating the data, (iii) limiting access to the information to only certain personnel of the other party, and/or (iv) using third-party intermediaries to aggregate or filter the data.

Issues may arise frequently with respect to the following types of information:

- **Current prices or trends in prices.** Historical financial information that will be part of any due diligence investigation will include revenues and sales volumes. Parties should not go beyond what is required for purposes of legitimate due diligence, and should avoid current pricing information whenever possible. If it is necessary for the buyer to obtain such information, consider limiting its circulation to only those who must see it, and preferably not to those engaged in competitive activities of the buyer.

- **Future pricing plans or marketing strategies.** Those assigned to evaluate the acquisition opportunity are being asked to judge the value, not of the target's past, but of its future performance. Information about what the target's management sees down the road for the business, and how it plans to respond to the challenges the target's business will face may seem like a necessary factor to consider before committing to the proposed acquisition. Unfortunately, detailed information on future plans, particularly with regard to pricing, is extremely risky to share when the prospective buyer and seller compete; it is exactly the kind of information the parties would exchange if their objective were to fix prices or allocate customers or markets. Again, information of this type should be provided to as few people as possible—or instead to outside accountants or investment bankers under strict confidentiality obligations—and not to those engaged in competitive activities of the buyer.

- **Customer-specific pricing or marketing information.** While aggregated historical information about prices and costs will be part of the data about the performance of the business which forms the basis of the due diligence investigation, information about the price charged to a particular customer generally should not be divulged by the target or sought by the potential acquirer. Exchange of customer-specific information may suggest an intention to fix prices to that customer. In general, the most highly sensitive cost and price information should be aggregated or otherwise masked to remove the commercial sensitivity.

- **Reciprocal exchanges of information, in the case of an acquisition (rather than a merger or joint venture).** If a buyer is evaluating the possible acquisition of a seller, or of a division or subsidiary of the seller, there may be no legitimate reason for the buyer to divulge sensitive information to the seller. Such a disclosure will only give rise to an implication that the parties are exchanging information for an inappropriate purpose. If the transaction involves a merger, or if the seller is receiving the buyer's shares as consideration, some due diligence regarding the buyer's business may be justified.

- **Counsel also can minimize antitrust risks by excluding certain personnel from exchanges of competitively sensitive information.** The negotiating team should be formed with the understanding that there is some risk that, at some point in the future, other parties may seek to characterize the discussions between the parties as evidence of an agreement in violation of

Section 1. For that reason, personnel with marketing responsibilities, or whose job responsibilities otherwise include the setting of prices, should not be part of the negotiating team unless this cannot be avoided.

In some cases there may simply be no way to evaluate the acquisition without taking into consideration competitively sensitive information.[32] One possible solution in such a case is to arrange for certain disclosures to be made "stepwise," so that the closer the parties come to signing and closing the deal, the more detailed and sensitive the disclosures that can be made. In addition, the competitively sensitive information can be disclosed to a "clean team," which may include an independent third party: An independent accountant to analyze financial information, for example, or an independent engineer to study and evaluate intellectual property, or retired or former employees with knowledge of the relevant business. The clean team can convert the data to a form that will avoid antitrust problems, such as masking the identity of specific customers, before transmitting it to the prospective purchaser.

Counsel should plan at the outset how to handle due diligence documents if the deal fails. If negotiations end without concluding a deal, counsel should ensure that all due diligence materials are returned to their original source and all copies destroyed.

---

[32] *See, e.g.*, United States v. Computer Assocs., Inc., Civil Action No. 01-02062 (D.D.C. Apr. 23, 2002) (permitted provision of customer bid information where there was a legitimate business need for access to such information, such as the proper valuation of the business based on future orders or orders in the pipeline), *available at* www.usdoj.gov/atr/cases/f11000/11083.pdf.

C. "We have agreed to acquire another company — what measures can we take to plan for integration or to ensure that the seller does not diminish the value of the business before closing?"

As stated previously, the HSR Act requires parties to wait at least thirty days (fifteen days in the case of a cash tender offer or acquisitions subject to bankruptcy court approval) before consummating their transaction unless the waiting period is terminated earlier. The purpose of the HSR Act is to maintain the competitive status quo while the agencies are given an opportunity to review prospective transactions for possible competitive problems and to decide whether to challenge them, or to require some corrective action to be taken prior to clearance (such as asset divestitures). As a consequence, parties must take care to avoid "jumping the gun" on the expiration of the HSR waiting period by agreeing to restrictions upon the seller that change the status quo during the waiting period and that can be seen as a transfer of beneficial ownership to the buyer prior to HSR approval. Obviously, this concern disappears once HSR approval is granted.

Moreover, parties to a proposed transaction remain separate entities until the actual closing. Where the parties to the proposed transaction are competitors, preclosing coordination of activity can be seen to violate the Sherman Act if the parties effectively stop competing against each other. This concern survives HSR approval, and applies until the transaction is in fact closed and the parties lose their separate identities.

At the same time, businesspeople often are justifiably concerned that the value of the asset being purchased can be lost or diminished during the period after signing but before closing, when the nominal owner of the asset may have different incentives than its future owner. Moreover, business people often perceive the need to "hit the ground running" on the day of closing. To do so, preclosing integration planning is often necessary.

This is one of the most challenging issues that company counsel can face: How can the integration needs (real and perceived) of the combining businesses be accommodated and how can the value of the deal be protected during the preclosing period without crossing the lines?

The FTC and the DOJ take preclosing coordination issues very seriously. For example, in 2003, Gemstar and TV Guide (who, prior to their merger in 2000, were competing producers of interactive program guides) settled gun-jumping charges brought by the DOJ by agreeing to pay $5.6 million in civil penalties, a record penalty for gun jumping.[33] The DOJ's complaint alleged that, prior to the closing of their merger in July 2000, and before the HSR Act waiting period had expired, the companies essentially combined their businesses through various actions. According to the DOJ, Gemstar and TV Guide agreed to allocate markets and customers between them and to fix prices and material terms offered to customers.

Similarly, provisions which give one party what amounts to veto power over the business operations of another party create substantial antitrust risk. For example, in 2002, the DOJ announced that it had settled charges against Computer Associates International, Inc. and Platinum Technology International, Inc. based on those parties' pre-HSR approval and preclosing conduct in connection with their 1999 merger.[34] The DOJ based its complaint on the fact that, among other things, Platinum was required to get Computer Associates' approval before it (i) offered discounts of more than 20 percent off list price; (ii) varied the terms of customer contracts from the pre-existing standard contract; (iii) offered consulting services for more than 30 days at a fixed price; and (iv) entered into Y2K remediation services. In addition, Computer Associates received information identifying Platinum's potential customers and the specific price, discount, and other contract terms offered to each customer and exercised management authority over day-to-day decisions like revenue recognition policies.

Significantly, in both *Computer Associates* and *Gemstar-TV Guide*, the DOJ charged violations of *both* the HSR waiting period requirements *and* Section 1 of the Sherman Act. In other words, the DOJ found that the preclosing conduct in question implicated both the gun-jumping concerns of the HSR Act and the general competition concerns of the Sherman Act.

---

[33] United States v. Gemstar-TV Guide Int'l, Civil Action No. 1:03CV00198 (D.D.C. Feb. 6, 2003), *available at* www.usdoj.gov/atc/cases/gemstar0.htm.

[34] *Computer Assocs.*, *supra* note 32.

Notwithstanding the above, parties are permitted to engage in preclosing planning activities to prepare for the postclosing environment, and to share information in connection with legitimate due diligence and preclosing planning.[35] In addition, concerns over gun jumping should not prevent parties from agreeing to provisions that obligate the seller to continue to operate in the ordinary course of business, but which do not require the buyer to approve any particular business conduct of the seller. Similarly, transactions that require the seller to maintain the corporate governance status quo are permissible. These provisions are routine and are simply designed to prevent the seller from taking actions during the waiting period that could seriously impair its value, and should not be deemed to enable the buyer to exercise control over the business operations of the buyer. Consequently, standard provisions, such as those that prohibit a seller, without the consent of the buyer, from increasing the compensation of directors or officers (except in the ordinary course of business), transferring or acquiring assets or settling claims or other similar provisions, should not run afoul of the HSR Act.

D. "We are planning a joint venture (or strategic alliance) with our competitor — what do we need to know?"

The terms "joint venture" and "strategic alliance" are used to describe a variety of business transactions. For antitrust purposes, the label applied to a transaction is secondary to determining its actual competitive effects. It is well settled that merely labeling an agreement with a competitor a joint venture or strategic alliance will not save it from prosecution under Section 1 of the Sherman Act if the purpose and effect of the agreement is to fix prices, restrict output, or allocate customers or geographic markets.[36] Naked price fixing agreements are, of course, per se violations of the antitrust laws. A competitor collaboration will be judged under the rule of reason, however, if it

---

35 *See supra* note 30.

36 Timken Roller Bearing Co. v. United States, 341 U.S. 593, 598 (1951).

involves sufficient integration of the activities of the parties to the transaction to produce efficiencies that will benefit competition.[37]

In April 2000, the FTC and DOJ jointly issued Antitrust Guidelines for Collaborations Among Competitors to provide the agencies' latest guidance on joint ventures.[38] In the guidelines, the agencies first examine the nature and business purpose of the agreement to determine whether the arrangement has the potential to harm competition. If not, the inquiry ends. If anticompetitive harm appears possible, the agencies attempt to determine the market(s) that the joint venture will affect. This market analysis begins with the definition of markets and calculations of market shares much in the way that merger review begins. The agencies will estimate whether the joint venture will create or facilitate the use of market power, especially if the parties to the joint venture might otherwise have acted independently. The agencies also will evaluate whether entry by other participants or other market factors will foster or impede competition. If this more detailed analysis indicates little or no potential for anticompetitive harm, the investigation will be closed. If such harm is possible, the agencies will weigh the procompetitive benefits of the joint venture against its anticompetitive effects.

Research and Development (R&D) and Production Joint Ventures. R&D joint ventures generally have been treated favorably by antitrust enforcement authorities when the participants continue to market independently the technologies or products that result from the venture. R&D ventures also often require substantial risk sharing and integration, which leads to procompetitive efficiencies such as economies of scale, pooling of complementary technologies, and cost

---

37 Broadcast Music, Inc. v. CBS, 441 U.S. 1, 20–21 (1979); *see also* Arizona v. Maricopa County Med. Soc'y, 457 U.S. 332, 356–57 (1982) (price-fixing agreement among competing physicians struck down as *per se* illegal due, in part, to the absence of integrative efficiencies such as capital pooling and risk sharing).

38 U.S. DEP'T OF JUSTICE & FEDERAL TRADE COMM'N ANTITRUST GUIDELINES FOR COLLABORATIONS AMONG COMPETITORS (2000), *reprinted in* 4 Trade Reg. Rep. (CCH) ¶ 13,161 [hereinafter COMPETITOR COLLABORATIONS GUIDELINES].

sharing. R&D ventures may raise antitrust concerns, however, if they have the potential to retard the pace of innovation.[39] Production joint ventures pose some additional antitrust risk, but also are likely to lead to efficiencies such as the ability to manufacture a new or improved product. The courts and the enforcement agencies have viewed production joint ventures favorably where the parties make appropriate assurances that they will continue to compete in the sale of the venture's output.[40]

Limited civil antitrust liability protection for R&D and production joint ventures is available under the National Cooperative Research and Production Act of 1993 (NCRPA).[41] The NCRPA mandates that R&D or production joint ventures[42] be judged under the rule of reason. In addition, the NCRPA limits to single damages state and federal antitrust damage awards against R&D and production joint ventures that notify the federal agencies of their arrangements and do not extend beyond the notified conduct.[43]

---

39 *See* DOJ and FTC ANTITRUST GUIDELINES FOR THE LICENSING OF INTELLECTUAL PROPERTY (1995) *reprinted in* 4 Trade Reg. Rep. (CCH) ¶ 13,132 [hereinafter INTELLECTUAL PROPERTY GUIDELINES]. The *Intellectual Property Guidelines* describe a rule of reason analysis to determine whether an R&D venture will reduce "innovation market" competition: "An innovation market consists of the research and development directed to particular new or improved goods or processes, and the close substitutes for that research and development." *Id.* § 3.2.3.

40 *See, e.g.*, General Motors Corp., 103 F.T.C. 374 (1984) (joint production venture between first and fourth largest auto manufacturers in the United States and Canada to produce a new model approved in part because the venture parents would continue to compete freely in the marketing of automobiles); United States v. Alcan Aluminum Ltd., 605 F. Supp. 619 (W.D. Ky. 1985) (joint production venture between competing firm approved due to safeguards against joint price and output decisions by the venture's parents).

41 15 U.S.C. §§ 4301–05.

42 The term "joint venture" is defined in 15 U.S.C. § 4301 (a).

43 15 U.S.C. § 4305.

Joint Selling or Marketing Arrangements. Joint selling or marketing arrangements between competitors, particularly those that prohibit the venture members from selling outside the venture and provide for centralized joint pricing and output decisions, have the potential to raise more serious antitrust concerns. These risks can be minimized by ensuring that the resources of the venture participants are truly integrated. For example, if a joint venture generates efficiencies, such as the ability to market a product that the participants could not have sold on their own, the venture's procompetitive virtues may outweigh its anticompetitive effects.[44] Antitrust risks also can be reduced by making any joint selling agreement between competitors nonexclusive.[45]

Joint Purchasing Arrangements. Joint purchasing arrangements generally are judged under the rule of reason due to the significant economies of scale they can generate.[46] However, joint purchasing arrangements between competitors that account for a large percentage of the purchasing market may be unlawful.[47] The antitrust concern is that a joint purchasing venture whose members account for a significant percentage of purchases in a market may be able to exercise monopsony power (the ability to drive prices below competitive levels). The *Health Care Statements* provide helpful guidance to firms contemplating a joint purchasing arrangement. There, the agencies established a safe harbor from antitrust prosecution for joint purchasing arrangements that (i) account for less than 35 percent of the total sales of the product or service in question, and (ii) involve products whose costs constitute less

---

44 *See, e.g.*, *Broadcast Music, Inc.*, 441 U.S. at 23.

45 *See, e.g.*, *id.* at 23–24.

46 *See* Northwest Wholesale Stationers v. Pacific Stationery & Printing Co., 472 U.S. 284, 295 (1984).

47 *See, e.g.*, Nat'l Macaroni Mfrs. Ass'n, 65 F.T.C. 583 (1964), *aff'd*, 345 F.2d 421 (7th Cir. 1965) (association of pasta producers violated Section 1 of the Sherman Act by manipulating and stabilizing prices by agreeing on the type of wheat they purchased to produce macaroni).

than 20 percent of the total revenues from all products and services sold by each of the venture's participants.[48]

Fully Integrated Joint Ventures. Ventures that integrate all aspects of two businesses are subject to the same analysis as mergers under Section 7 of the Clayton Act.[49] The federal antitrust enforcement agencies have challenged fully integrated joint ventures on the grounds that they would eliminate potential competition between the venture participants in highly concentrated markets[50] or limit access to downstream competitors.[51] Joint ventures that lead to the formation of a new entity, the voting securities of which will be acquired by the parents, may be subject to HSR premerger notification requirements.[52]

Beyond the structure of the joint venture, collateral restraints—agreements that further restrain competition between joint venture participants—on price, output, customers, or territories may

---

48 US DEP'T OF JUSTICE & FEDERAL TRADE COMM'N, STATEMENTS OF ENFORCEMENT POLICY AND ANALYTICAL PRINCIPLES RELATING TO HEALTH CARE, *reprinted in* 4 Trade Reg. Rep. (CCH) ¶ 13,153 (Sept. 5, 1996) [hereinafter HEALTH CARE STATEMENTS].

49 15 U.S.C. § 18. *See* discussion, *supra*, for a discussion of Section 7 of the Clayton Act and merger analysis. An issue that may arise in the analysis of a fully integrated venture is whether full integration was necessary to achieve the efficiencies driving the transaction. United States v. Ivaco, Inc., 704 F. Supp. 1409, 1426 (W.D. Mich. 1989).

50 *See* United States v. Penn-Olin Chem. Corp., 378 U.S. 158 (1964) (joint venture formed to set up a chlorate plant might violate Section 7 if it eliminated threat of potential separate entry by both of the venture participants); Yamaha Motor Co. v. F.T.C., 657 F.2d 971 (8th Cir. 1981); (joint venture between outboard motor manufacturers unlawful because it eliminated a potential competitor in a highly concentrated market.).

51 *See, e.g.*, United States v. MCI Communication Corp., 1994-2 Trade Cus. (CCH) ¶ 70,730 (D.D.C. 1994) (joint venture between dominant U.K. telecommunications carrier and second largest U.S. long-distance carrier gave venture participants the incentive to favor each other over competing carriers with respect to necessary service interconnections).

52 15 U.S.C. § 18a.

separately violate Section 1 of the Sherman Act. In general, collateral restraints that are ancillary to a legitimate business objective of the venture or alliance will be judged under the rule of reason.[53] The *Competitor Collaborations Guidelines* require that a restraint adopted as ancillary to a joint venture be "reasonably related to the integration and reasonably necessary to achieve its procompetitive benefits."[54]

On the other hand, collateral restraints that have no legitimate purpose, such as price fixing, may be found to violate Section 1 of the Sherman Act without a detailed rule of reason analysis.[55] In order to avoid per se condemnation, collateral restraints should be (i) undertaken by a bona fide joint venture, and (2) reasonably necessary to the venture's legitimate purpose.[56]

Excluding other competitors from a joint venture or alliance may run afoul of the antitrust laws if access to the venture is essential to compete effectively in the marketplace and there are no legitimate business

---

53 *See* SCFC ILC, Inc. v. VISA USA, Inc., 36 F.3d 958, 970 (10th Cir. 1994), (collateral restraints must be "reasonably related to . . . and no broader than necessary to effectuate," the procompetitive purpose of the venture); NCAA v. Board of Regents, 468 U.S. 85, 109–10 (1984); Arizona v. Maricopa County Med. Soc'y, 457 U.S. 332, 356–57 (1982).

54 *See* COMPETITOR COLLABORATIONS GUIDELINES, *supra* note 38 § 3.2; *see also* HEALTH CARE STATEMENTS, *supra* note 48, Statement 7.B.2 (requiring that collateral agreements contained in certain joint ventures be "reasonably necessary" to achieve stated efficiencies); INTELLECTUAL PROPERTY GUIDELINES, *supra* note 39 § 4.2 (considering whether "restraint in a licensing arrangement" is "reasonably necessary to achieve procompetitive benefits").

55 NCAA v. Bd. of Regents, 468 U.S. 85, 109–10 (1984); *see also* Arizona v. Maricopa County Med. Soc'y, 457 U.S. 332, 356–57 (1982).

56 *Broadcast Music, Inc.*, 441 U.S. at 23 (price restraint accompanying blanket licenses to musical compositions upheld because (i) it was accompanied by integration of sales, monitoring, and enforcement against copyright infringement; and (ii) restraint was necessary in order to "market the product at all"); *see also* National Bancard v. VISA USA, Inc., 779 F.2d 592 (11th Cir.) (1986) (joint bank credit card interchange fees system was central to the continued existence of the product).

reasons for denying access.[57] Preventing firms from "free riding" on the investments of venture participants may be an example of a legitimate justification for exclusion.

57 *See, e.g.*, *Northwest Wholesale Stationers*, 472 U.S. at 284.

E. "Where can I go for more information?"

A. "We are contemplating merging with or acquiring another company — what sort of antitrust approvals will we need?"

- ABA SECTION OF ANTITRUST LAW, THE MERGER REVIEW PROCESS: A STEP-BY-STEP GUIDE TO FEDERAL MERGER REVIEW (2001).
- US DEP'T OF JUSTICE & FEDERAL TRADE COMM'N, 1992 HORIZONTAL MERGER GUIDELINES, *reprinted in* 4 Trade Reg. Rep. (CCH) ¶ 13,104 (Apr. 17, 1997).
- NAAG HORIZONTAL MERGER GUIDELINES, *reprinted in* 4 Trade Reg. Rep. (CCH) ¶ 13,405 (Apr. 13, 1993).

B. "We're going forward with a merger or acquisition — what can we talk about during due diligence?"

- ABA SECTION OF ANTITRUST LAW, A PRIMER ON THE LAW OF INFORMATION EXCHANGE (2d ed. 2002).
- William Blumenthal, *The Scope of Permissible Coordination Between Merging Entities Prior to Consummation,* 63 ANTITRUST L.J. 1 (1994).
- Ilene Knable Gotts & Michael B. Miller, *Information Sharing and Joint Activities in the Pre-Consummation Context: How to Plan for the Post-Transition Entity,* ANTITRUST REPORT 2 (March 1999).

C. "We have agreed to acquire another company — what measures can we take to plan for integration or to ensure that the seller does not diminish the value of the business before closing?"

- ABA SECTION OF ANTITRUST LAW, A PRIMER ON THE LAW OF INFORMATION EXCHANGE (2d ed. 2002).

- William Blumenthal, *The Scope of Permissible Coordination Between Merging Entities Prior to Consummation*, 63 ANTITRUST L.J. 1 (1994).
- Ilene Knable Gotts & Michael B. Miller, *Information Sharing and Joint Activities in the Pre-Consummation Context: How to Plan for the Post-Transition Entity,* ANTITRUST REPORT 2 (March 1999).

D. "We are planning a joint venture (or strategic alliance) with our competitor — what do we need to know?"

- US DEP'T OF JUSTICE & FEDERAL TRADE COMM'N, ANTITRUST GUIDELINES FOR COLLABORATIONS AMONG COMPETITORS (2000), *reprinted in* 4 Trade Reg. Rep. (CCH) ¶ 13,161 (Apr. 2000).
- DOJ AND FTC ANTITRUST GUIDELINES FOR THE LICENSING OF INTELLECTUAL PROPERTY (1995) *reprinted in* 4 Trade Reg. Rep. (CCH) ¶ 13,132 (Apr. 6, 1995).
- US DEP'T OF JUSTICE & FEDERAL TRADE COMM'N, STATEMENTS OF ENFORCEMENT POLICY AND ANALYTICAL PRINCIPLES RELATING TO HEALTH CARE, *reprinted in* 4 Trade Reg. Rep. (CCH) ¶ 13,153 (Sept. 5, 1996).

CHAPTER III

ROBINSON-PATMAN ACT AND PRICE DISCRIMINATION

A. "Can we charge one of our best customers a lower price? They will pick up the product at our factory, and every other competitor is offering them a discount."

Section 2 of the Clayton Act,[1] as amended by the Robinson-Patman Act,[2] prohibits the sale of two products of like grade and quality at different prices to two different buyers where the price difference may result in injury to competition. The Robinson-Patman Act is violated if

- The goods involved in either the sale to the "favored customer" or the sale to a competing "disfavored customer" are "in commerce." If the goods in one of the two transactions cross a state line, the goods are deemed to be "in commerce."[3]
- The buyers pay different prices.[4] "Price" under Section 2(a) is the ultimate purchase price, net of all discounts, rebates, allowances, payment terms, and credits.[5]

---

1 15 U.S.C. § 13.

2 Act of June 19, 1936, 15 U.S.C. §§ 13–13b, 21a. Section 1 of the Robinson-Patman Act is codified as § 2 of the Clayton Act.

3 *See, e.g.*, Gulf Oil Corp. v. Copp Paving Co., 419 U.S. 186, 195 (1974).

4 *See, e.g.*, F.T.C. v. Anheuser-Busch, Inc., 363 U.S. 2d 536, 549 (1960).

5 *See, e.g.*, Conoco Inc. v. Inman Oil Co., 774 F.2d 895, 901–02 (8th Cir. 1985).

- A single seller makes at least two completed sales to different purchasers.[6]
- The products are of "like grade and quality." Products meet this test if they have the same (or similar) physical and performance characteristics. Differences in brand name, packaging, or labeling of the products do not sufficiently distinguish them for purposes of the Act.[7]
- The "products" in question are tangible goods, not intangible items such as services.[8] Mixed transactions involving goods and services are considered tangible goods if the goods component of the package "predominates."[9]
- The transactions must be sales. The Act does not apply to leases, consignments, or product swaps.[10]
- The price differential may lessen competition. Competitive injury may occur at the "primary line" of the distribution chain (where the alleged victim is a competitor of the seller) or at the "secondary line" of the distribution chain (if the injured party is a competitor of the favored buyer). In a primary line case, the evidence must show injury to competition (as opposed to a single competitor) due to predatory pricing by the seller.[11] Proof of injury in a secondary line case requires a showing of competition between the favored and disfavored buyers. Thus, there can be

---

6 The two completed sales also must be reasonably contemporaneous in time. *See, e.g.*, Airweld, Inc. v Airco, Inc., 742 F.2d 1184, 1191 (9th Cir. 1984).

7 *See, e.g.*, F.T.C. v. Borden Co., 383 U.S. 637, 639–47 (1996).

8 *See, e.g.*, Metro Communications Co. v. Ameritech Mobile Communications, Inc., 984 F.2d 739, 745 (6th Cir. 1993) (cellular telephone service not a commodity).

9 *See, e.g.*, First Comics, Inc. v. World Color Press, Inc., 884 F.2d 1033 (7th Cir. 1989).

10 *See, e.g.*, Export Liquor Sales, Inc. v. Ammex Warehouse Co., 426 F.2d 251, 252 (6th Cir. 1970) (leases); Rebel Oil Co. v. Atlantic Richfield Oil Co., 146 F.3d 1088, 1094 (9th Cir. 1998) (swaps).

11 *See, e.g.*, Brooke Group v. Brown & Williamson Corp., 509 U.S. 209, 221–22 (1993).

no secondary line injury where the two buyers compete for different sets of customers or in different geographic markets.[12] The courts of appeal are split on whether injury to a single competitor is sufficient to establish competitive injury in a secondary line case.[13] A strong inference of injury to competition arises when a substantial price differential for a product resold in the same form is maintained over time in a keenly competitive industry.[14]

A "prima facie" case of price discrimination will be established if all these elements are satisfied; however, numerous defenses might be available.

A "cost justification" defense to price discrimination is available where the seller can show that the discount it provided to the buyer was not greater than the savings the seller enjoyed because the buyer purchased certain quantities of product or purchased through certain methods.[15] Volume discounts may qualify for the cost justification defense if the seller can establish that the additional volume purchased allowed it to reduce its manufacturing, selling, or delivery costs, but not

---

12 *See, e.g.*, Best Brands Beverage, Inc. v. Falstaff Brewing Corp., 842 F.2d, 578, 585–86 (2d Cir. 1987) (no finding of competitive injury because purchasers operated in different territories and did not compete).

13 *Compare* George Haug Co., Inc. v. Rolls Royce Motor Cars, Inc., 148 F.3d 136, 143–44 (2d Cir. 1998) (injury to a single competitor sufficient to establish secondary line competitive injury); Chroma Lighting v. GTE Prods. Corp., 111 F.3d 653, 658 (9th Cir. 1997) (same); Coastal Fuels of Puerto Rico, Inc. v. Caribbean Petroleum Corp., 79 F.3d 182, 189 (1st Cir. 1996) (same); J.F. Feeser, Inc. v. Serv-A-Portion, Inc., 904 F.2d 1524 (3d Cir. 1990) (same); *with* Boise Cascade Corp. v. F.T.C., 837 F.2d 1127, 1144 (D.C. Cir. 1988) (injury to competition required for secondary line violation); Richard Short Oil Co. v. Texaco, Inc., 799 F.2d 415, 420 (8th Cir. 1986) (same); Motive Parts Warehouse v. Facet Enters., 774 2d 380, 393-95 (10th Cir. 1985) (same).

14 Texaco, Inc. v. Hasbrouck, 496 U.S. 543, 559 (1990); F.T.C. v. Morton Salt Co., 334 U.S. 37, 50 (1948).

15 15 U.S.C. § 13(a).

otherwise.[16] Such cost savings can be passed on to the buyer in the form of a discount, so long as the discount does not exceed the savings to the seller. For example, a customer that agrees to pick up a purchased product at the seller's factory may be eligible for a greater discount, provided that the discount is equal to or less than the delivery costs avoided by the seller.[17] The seller has the burden of proving the cost justification defense through a prediscount cost study that demonstrates the savings generated by the sale to the favored purchaser. The requirement that the cost study must be undertaken in advance of the discount has limited the utility of this defense.

The "meeting competition" defense permits a seller to offer discriminatory discounts to meet the "equally low price of a competitor."[18] This defense requires the seller to have a good faith basis for meeting the competitive offer. The seller must receive information about the competitive offer from a reliable source, typically the customer to whom the offer was made.[19] Attempts by the seller to verify a price through direct contact with a competitor, however, may be construed as evidence of a price-fixing agreement and can therefore lead to liability under Section 1 of the Sherman Act.[20] As a consequence, a seller wishing to meet a competitor's offer should make specific inquiries to the customer to determine key terms of the competitive offer such as the identity of the competitor, nature of the product, the price or discount offered, and the duration of the offer. The seller should try to get this information in writing, and if not available, contemporaneously record this information (including its source) in preparation for a possible challenge to its differential price.[21] A seller may respond to a

---

16 *See, e.g.*, Acadia Motors, Inc. v. Ford Motor Co., 844 F. Supp. 819, 831 (D. Me. 1994), *aff'd in part and rev'd in part on other grounds*, 44 F.3d 1050 (1st Cir. 1995).

17 *See Morton Salt Co.*, 334 U.S. at 48.

18 15 U.S.C. § 13(b).

19 *See* Great Atl. & Pac. Tea Co. v. F.T.C., 440 U.S. 69, 82 (1979).

20 United States v. United States Gypsum Co., 438 U.S. 442, 451 (1978).

21 *See* Reserve Supply Corp. v. Owens-Corning Fiberglass Corp., 971 F.2d 37, 40–48 (7th Cir. 1992).

competitor's price across an entire area such as a state or region.[22] The defense may be used to retain an existing customer or to gain a new one. The seller's price may be reduced to meet the competitor's price, but not to beat it. In some unusual situations an equal price may in fact "beat" the competitor's price, once quality differences are considered. Finally, the defense is available even if the seller elects to meet competing offers to some customers, but not others.[23]

A lower price also may be justified by proof that the favored buyer performed a "function" that relieved the seller of costs or raised the buyer's costs. Like the cost justification defense, the functional discount defense allows the seller to pass along cost savings generated by a buyer that performs certain functions for the seller so long as the savings and the discount are reasonably related. The discount may reflect the savings to the seller, the value of the services to the seller, or additional costs incurred by the buyer. The functional discount defense may, for example, justify the grant of a lower price to a wholesaler than to the retailer of the same product.[24]

An "availability" defense can be asserted if the lower price offered to the favored buyer is, as a practical matter, available to the disfavored buyer but that buyer fails to take advantage of it. A discount is functionally available to a disfavored buyer if (1) the disfavored buyer knew about the offer, and (2) the lower price was actually, not just theoretically, available to the disfavored purchaser. A "sales growth" or "share of shelf space" discount normally meet these conditions. A volume discount program, for example, might not be actually available to a purchaser unable to purchase enough volume to earn the discount.[25]

---

22 Falls City Indus. v. Vanco Beverage, Inc., 460 U.S. 428, 441 (1983).

23 *Id.* at 455.

24 *Hasbrouck*, 496 U.S. at 561. For guidelines on using functional discounts as a defense to a Section 2(a) claim, see David A. Hemminger, *Cost Justification—A Defense With New Applications*, 59 ANTITRUST L.J. 827, 846–48 (1991).

25 *Morton Salt Co.*, 334 U.S. at 42 (quantity discount was not functionally available to individual customers that could not purchase enough volume to qualify for the quantity discounts enjoyed by larger customers).

However, a minimum purchase requirement well within the means of the average dealer may not be considered discriminatory.[26]

A defense of "changing conditions" due to "actual or imminent deterioration of perishable goods, obsolescence of seasonal goods, distress sales under court process, or sales in good faith in discontinuance" of the business relating to the goods may justify a lower price to one customer.[27] The courts have upheld the "changing conditions" defense in situations involving outdated automobile models,[28] perishable fresh foods,[29] and technological obsolescence.[30]

B. "Can we help one of our best customers with some extra advertising support?"

In addition to prohibiting price discrimination, the Robinson-Patman Act requires a seller to make promotional allowances and services in connection with the resale of the seller's products "available on proportionally equal terms to all customers competing in the distribution of such products."[31] "Promotional allowances and services" include various forms of nonprice support to customers, such as cooperative advertising support, handbills, demonstrations, catalogs, displays, prizes for promotional contests, special packaging, or anything else used to support product resale. The alleged discriminatory promotional

---

26 *See* Bouldis v. U.S. Suzuki Motor Corp., 711 F.2d 1319, 1326 (6th Cir. 1983) (minimum of four to eight motorcycles).

27 15 U.S.C. § 13(a).

28 Valley Plymouth v. Studebaker-Packard Corp., 219 F. Supp. 608 (S.D. Cal. 1963).

29 A.A. Poultry Farms v. Rose Acre Farms, 686 F. Supp. 680, 691 (S.D. Ind. 1988), *aff'd on other grounds,* 881 F.2d 1396 (7th Cir. 1989).

30 *See, e.g.*, Comcoa, Inc. v. NEC Tels., Inc., 931 F.2d 655 (10th Cir. 1991).

31 15 U.S.C. § 13(d), (e). Section 2(d) addresses "promotional allowances." Section 2(e) refers to "services." The main difference between the two concepts is who pays for the promotion—the product seller or the buyer. This analysis applies whether the product seller supplies the promotional material or pays the buyer to supply it.

programs must be reasonably contemporaneous to run afoul of this provision of the Act.

As stated earlier, no violation will be found if the promotional allowances are available to all on "proportionally equal terms." In order to be "available" to customers for purposes of these sections, the availability of the seller's program(s) should be communicated in writing to all competing customers. The FTC has advised that firms offering promotional allowances should provide their customers with sufficient information to make an informed decision whether to participate.[32] The promotional allowances offered to competing buyers need not be identical in form or content, only "proportional." Unfortunately, there is no simple test to determine whether allowances or services are available on "proportionally equal terms." This is essentially a question of fact. The FTC guidelines on this subject, commonly referred to as the "Fred Meyer Guides," advise that one accepted method of ensuring proportionality is to offer allowances and services as a percentage of the customer's purchases or sales of the seller's products.[33] The proportional availability requirements of Sections 2(d) and (e) also apply to promotional allowances offered to indirect purchasers that resell the manufacturer's products, such as retailers that buy from a distributor.[34]

The "meeting competition" defense discussed in the previous section is the only defense available for discrimination in promotional allowances and services. The same elements apply as those for price discrimination. A seller may therefore offer favorable allowances or services to a particular customer if the offer was necessary to meet a competitive offer.

---

32 *Guides For Advertising Allowances and Other Merchandising Payments and Services (Fred Meyer Guides)*, 16 C.F.R. § 240.10(b).

33 *Id.* § 240.9; *see also* Alan's of Atlanta v. Minolta Corp., 903 F.2d 1414, 1423–24 (11th Cir. 1990) (allowances not proportionally equal where disfavored customer received only one half as much in allowance funds per units it purchased).

34 F.T.C. v. Fred Meyer, Inc., 390 U.S. 341, 358 (1968).

C. "Where can I go for more information?"

A. "Can we charge one of our best customers a lower price? They will pick up the product at our factory and every other competitor is offering them a discount."

- ANTITRUST LAW DEVELOPMENTS (FIFTH) at 455–523.
- ABA SECTION OF ANTITRUST LAW, MONOGRAPH NO. 4, THE ROBINSON-PATMAN ACT: POLICY AND LAW (1980, 1983).

B. "Can we help one of our best customers with some extra advertising support?"

- ANTITRUST LAW DEVELOPMENTS (FIFTH) at 455–523.
- *Guides for Advertising Allowances and Other Merchandising Payments and Services (Fred Meyer Guides)*, 16 C.F.R. § 240 (2003).

CHAPTER IV

DEALING WITH CUSTOMERS AND SUPPLIERS

A. "Our distributor's pricing and advertising are wrecking the marketplace — what can we do about it?"

Suppliers are often concerned that a reseller's low price can adversely affect other resellers and the supplier by discouraging the provision of services, eroding brand image, or jeopardizing the supplier's ability to introduce new products by depressing price points.

Setting Resale Prices.[1] Agreements between suppliers and resellers setting minimum resale prices or price levels are per se illegal under Section 1 of the Sherman Act. By contrast, vertical agreements that establish maximum or "ceiling" resale prices are judged under the rule of reason.[2]

However, even with respect to the setting of minimum resale price targets, a supplier may unilaterally adopt a "*Colgate* policy,"[3] pursuant to which it may simply announce a price at which its product must be resold and refuse to sell to any reseller that fails to comply. Minimum price policies give resellers sufficient margin to provide services and to enhance other aspects of the selling environment (such as ample

---

1 At the outset, it is important to understand that there may be regulatory impediments—apart from general antitrust concerns discussed below—to taking action against discounting distributors. For example, there may be state and federal franchisee, distributor, or dealer protection laws that may limit supplier options. Industry-specific and franchise statutes are beyond the scope of this discussion.

2 *See* State Oil Co. v. Khan, 522 U.S. 3, 18 (1997).

3 *See* United States v. Colgate & Co., 250 U.S. 300, 307 (1919).

inventory and showrooms) that are consistent with the supplier's objectives.[4]

Under the *Colgate* doctrine, announcing the terms upon which a seller will deal with a customer on a unilateral basis is not an agreement for Sherman Act purposes. Many manufacturers of branded products in industries such as consumer electronics, furniture, appliances, sporting goods, luggage, handbags, agricultural supplies, and automotive replacement parts have successfully implemented *Colgate* policies to reduce the discounting of their products.

The theory behind *Colgate* is that, where the supplier acts unilaterally, there is no concerted action present, and thus no Section 1 liability. However, where the supplier takes action that results in the distributor's or retailer's adherence to the pricing policy, the plurality requirement can be found to have been satisfied. Moreover, particularly difficult issues can arise where a supplier acts against a noncomplying reseller as the result of complaints received by those who comply. While merely acting on those complaints is not enough to establish the existence of concerted action,[5] it is important for the supplier to act independently of the complaining reseller, so as to avoid liability for a vertical refusal to deal in violation of Section 1 or for a price-fixing agreement between the supplier and the complaining reseller.[6]

Colgate pricing policies may be used broadly or selectively to cover everything from a single product to all of the supplier's offerings. They can be used in particular geographic areas or with specific channels of distribution where price erosion is a problem, or they can be used throughout the country or the supplier's distribution system. In each

---

4 Sales through agents and independent sales representatives (as well as bona fide consignment sales, *see, e.g.*, Simpson v. Union Oil Co., 377 U.S. 13, 21 (1964) are unilateral activities on the part of the supplier because title flows directly to the end-user from the supplier. These are outside the scope of Section 1 of the Sherman Act because there is no concerted activity involving more than one actor. *See* Copperweld Corp. v. Independence Tube Corp., 467 U.S. 752, 767–68 (1984).

5 *See* Monsanto Co. v. Spray-Rite Service Corp., 465 U.S. 752, 763–64 (1984).

6 *Id.* at 768.

case, a policy violation requires that the supplier stop selling the offending reseller the product or products involved or pull an entire product line or all of the supplier's products, regardless of whether their prices are all subject to the policy.

Colgate policies should be implemented with great care. There can be no written agreements containing minimum pricing terms, no conduct that seeks to compel or coerce adherence to the supplier's minimum pricing terms, and no second chances or "probation" for policy offenders.[7] Careful training and supervision of employees who interact with customers is therefore essential in order to strictly maintain the policy's unilateral (and thus lawful) quality.

Implementing a direct sales program is another option for a supplier concerned about discounted pricing of its products. Under such a program, the supplier sells to end-users directly or through agents.[8]

Promotional Programs. Suppliers also may encourage desirable pricing behavior by providing financial or other incentives. These practices are judged under the rule of reason because participation is not mandatory.[9] Promotional allowances also are subject to the Robinson-Patman Act.[10]

Firms often use cooperative advertising programs that encourage advertising at nondiscounted prices, commonly referred to as Minimum Advertised Price (MAP) programs. Under such programs, the reseller is free to set its own resale price, but receives an advertising allowance (typically in the form of cooperative advertising funds) only if advertising the product at or above a designated price. Many companies pay an explicit allowance (such as a three-percent rebate on purchases), while others, including several consumer electronics manufacturers, use

---

7 United States v. Parke, Davis & Co., 362 U.S. 29, 44 (1960).

8 State law may prohibit a manufacturer or supplier from selling directly to end-users. For example, state law typically prohibits producers from selling alcoholic beverages directly to consumers.

9 In 1987, the FTC announced that the rule of reason applies to price restrictions in promotional programs. *See* 6 Trade Reg. Rep. (CCH) ¶ 39,057 at 41,728 (F.T.C. May 21, 1987).

10 *See* discussion, *supra,* at pages 49–50.

an implicit allowance whereby the failure to follow the program results in a future price increase to the reseller for products covered by the program. Group or shared-price advertising whereby the manufacturer sponsors an advertisement listing sellers that agree to sell at the price listed in the advertisement is another form of cooperative advertising. Cooperative advertising programs are judged under the rule of reason because they usually do not restrain a reseller from selling at a discount or from advertising discounts when the reseller itself paid for the advertisement.[11]

Although MAP programs are generally viewed to be procompetitive or competitively neutral, they are nonetheless subject to antitrust attack if they go beyond restricting reimbursement for the advertisement of discounts. The FTC, for example, in an enforcement action against the five largest distributors of prerecorded music charged that the distributors' MAP policies that allegedly prohibited retailers from advertising discounts in all advertising, even advertising paid for entirely by the retailer, violated the FTC Act.[12]

B. "Can we require customers of our hot new product to buy some of our slow-selling old product?"

Conditioning the sale of one product on the purchase of another may constitute tying and be illegal if certain conditions are met. Courts have defined tying arrangements as "an agreement by a party to sell one product [the tying product] but only on the condition that the buyer also purchases a different (or tied) product."[13] Tying arrangements also may involve services[14] or leases.[15] Tying arrangements are per se illegal if the four conditions described below are met. Even if the four

---

11 *See, e.g.*, The Advertising Checking Bureau, Inc., 109 F.T.C. 146 (1987).

12 Sony Music Distrib. Inc., [F.T.C. Complaints & Orders 1997–2001 Transfer Binder] Trade Reg. Rep. (CCH) ¶ 24,746 (F.T.C. Aug. 30, 2000).

13 Northern Pac. Ry. v. United States, 356 U.S. 1, 5–6 (1958).

14 Jefferson Parish Hosp. Dist. No. 2 v. Hyde, 466 U.S. 2, 21 (1984).

15 United Shoe Mach. Corp. v. United States, 258 U.S. 451 (1922).

conditions are not met, the arrangement might still be condemned under the rule of reason.[16]

First, the arrangement must involve two separate products or services. The question whether there are two products must be answered from the perspective of a consumer, not a producer. Even if the products could be viewed as an integrated package, the proper question is whether the parts of the package could be "distinguishable in the eyes of buyers." [17] Thus, in *Jefferson Parish*, the court found that anesthesiological and inpatient acute care services were separate products because there was a "separate demand" for these services. Evidence that the two products or services are actually purchased separately can be persuasive, as in *Kodak,* where copier parts and copier service had been sold separately in the past.[18]

In *United States v. Microsoft*, the D.C. Circuit declined to apply the *Jefferson Parish* test of determining the existence of separate products by reference to the character of demand.[19] The D.C. Circuit concluded that "[i]f integration has efficiency benefits these may be ignored by the *Jefferson Parish* proxies. Because one cannot be sure beneficial integration will be protected by the other elements of the per se rule, simple application of that rule's separate-products test may make consumers worse off."[20] The court concluded that the per se rule should not be applied to the bundling of platform software products because the judiciary's experience with platform software tying arrangements was insufficient to permit a "comfortabl[e]" conclusion that bundling in platform software markets invariably harms competition.[21]

---

16 *See Jefferson Parish*, 466 U.S. at 34.

17 *Id.* at 19.

18 Eastman Kodak Co. v. Image Technical Servs., 504 U.S. 451 (1992).

19 253 F.3d 34, 84–97 (D.C. Cir. 2001) (en banc).

20 *Id.* at 89.

21 *Id.* at 94; *cf.* Arizona v. Maricopa County Med. Soc'y, 457 U.S. 332, 349 n.19 (1982) (rejecting view that it should not apply the per se rule because it had little antitrust experience in the health care industry).

Second, the sale of one product must be conditioned on the purchase of another. There can be no tie when the tying product is separately available to the buyer. The seller's pricing policy must avoid unreasonably high prices for separate purchases.[22] Courts have differed on the proof required to meet this "conditioning" requirement. Most courts have interpreted language in *Jefferson Parish*—"force the buyer into the purchase of tied product that the buyer . . . did not want at all"—as requiring some proof of coercion.[23] A minority do not see coercion as a required element, but only as evidence of market power, which is the third prerequisite to a per se tying violation.[24]

Third, the seller must have sufficient economic power in the tying product to produce an appreciable restraint in the market for the tied product. If the "hot-selling" product is not so hot after all, the tying arrangement will not be per se illegal. "Economic power" means that "the seller has some special ability—usually called 'market power'—to force a purchaser to do something that he would not do in a competitive market."[25] Although not conclusive, high market shares are usually indicative of market power. There is a general consensus that market power, however, is not to be presumed merely by virtue of the existence of a patent because patented goods, like nonpatented goods, may have substitutes. In *Kodak*,[26] the court found the possibility of sufficient market power in downstream markets even where there was no power in the market for original equipment. There, Kodak was accused of tying the sale of replacement parts for its product to the purchase of repair services. The court found the possibility of sufficient power in the market for parts, even if Kodak had no power in the market for copiers, because there might be sufficient Kodak copier owners who were

---

22 United States v. Loew's Inc., 371 U.S. 38, 52, 54–55 (1962).

23 Trans Sport, Inc. v. Starter Sportswear, Inc., 964 F.2d 186, 192 (2d Cir. 1992).

24 *See, e.g.*, Bell v. Cherokee Aviation Corp., 660 F.2d 1123, 1130–32 (6th Cir. 1981).

25 *Jefferson Parish,* 466 U.S. at 13.

26 504 U.S. at 476.

"locked in" to Kodak copiers and could not economically switch.[27] Most subsequent courts have construed this lock-in argument narrowly.[28]

Fourth, the arrangement must affect a "not insubstantial amount" of interstate commerce in the tied product. This test focuses on the absolute amount of commerce involved, not on the market share of the buyer or seller, and is usually considered a de minimis test. The Supreme Court has found amounts as small as $60,000 to be "not insubstantial."[29]

Even where not all of the four conditions for per se condemnation are met, an arrangement still may be found unlawful under the rule of reason if the arrangement has an "actual adverse effect on competition."[30] Alleged tying arrangements, however, are rarely condemned under the rule of reason. For example, in *Town Sound & Custom Tops, Inc. v. Chrysler Motors Corp.*,[31] the plaintiff alleged that Chrysler tied the sale of Chrysler radios to the purchase of Chrysler vehicles. The Third Circuit, after finding that the per se test had not been satisfied, ruled that Chrysler's conduct was lawful under the rule of reason because of the plaintiff's failure to set forth a plausible theory of how the inclusion of factory-installed radios as standard features in Chrysler vehicles caused competitive injury.[32]

Two other similar marketing arrangements—full line forcing and reciprocal dealing—have been analyzed using tying arrangement analysis.

Full line forcing, that is, requiring a distributor to stock the manufacturer's full line of products, generally has been found to be lawful under a tying analysis. These agreements usually do not explicitly prevent a distributor from selling other manufacturers' products; instead,

---

27 *Id.*

28 *See, e.g.*, Virtual Maint., Inc. v. Prime Computer, Inc., 11 F.3d 660, 666 (6th Cir. 1993).

29 *Loew's*, 371 U.S. at 38.

30 *Jefferson Parish*, 466 U.S. at 29.

31 959 F.2d 468 (3d Cir. 1992) (en banc).

32 *Id.* at 487.

they usually require that the distributor stock the "forcing" manufacturer's full line. If the effect is that the distributor has no more shelf space for a competitor manufacturer's products, then competition might be foreclosed. Courts in recent years have rarely condemned such arrangements.[33]

Reciprocal dealing, where one party buys goods from another only on the understanding that the second party will buy goods from the first, is usually found to be lawful under a tying analysis. The Supreme Court has never considered a reciprocal dealing case. Lower courts generally have used a tying analysis because the arrangement appears to be similar—a party with power, here a buyer, forces a seller to purchase a good or service it might not otherwise want.[34] Reciprocal dealing arrangements rarely have run afoul of the antitrust laws.[35]

---

33 *See, e.g.,* Smith Mach. Co. v. Hesston Corp., 878 F.2d 1290, 1295–98 (10th Cir. 1989).

34 Spartan Grain & Mill Co. v. Ayers, 581 F.2d 419, 425 (5th Cir. 1978).

35 The FTC, however, retains power to examine exclusive dealing under Section 5 of the Federal Trade Commission Act, 15 U.S.C. §45(a).

C. "Where can I go for more information?"

A. "Our distributor's pricing and advertising are wrecking the marketplace — what can we do about it?"

- ANTITRUST LAW DEVELOPMENTS (FIFTH) at 130–75.
- State Oil Co. *v.* Khan, 522 U.S. 3 (1997).
- Warren D. Grimes, *The Life Cycle of a Venerable Precedent: GTE Sylvania and the Future of Vertical Restraints Law*, ANTITRUST 27 (Fall 2002).
- Brian R. Henry & Eugene F. Zelek, Jr., *A Colgate How-To: Establishing and Maintaining an Effective Minimum Resale Price Policy*, ANTITRUST 8 (Summer 2003).

B. "Can we require customers of our hot new product to buy some of our slow-selling old product?"

- ANTITRUST LAW DEVELOPMENTS (FIFTH) at 175–228.
- United States *v.* Microsoft Corp., 253 F.3d 34 (D.C. Cir. 2001).

CHAPTER V

DEALING WITH THE ANTITRUST AUTHORITIES IN THE UNITED STATES AND ABROAD

A. "Somebody from the Department of Justice (or the Federal Trade Commission or a State Attorney General's office) just called — what should I do?"

The proper response to any government inquiry depends on the nature of the inquiry itself. There are any number of situations in which an individual or company might be contacted by someone from the government. The contact could be the surprise execution of a search warrant in a criminal investigation, a demand for information related to a civil investigation, an attempt to gather information about the company as part of an agency study of an industry, or an informal contact to gather information about a transaction between other companies with which your client may do business or compete. Your client's response could be completely voluntary, or it could be compelled by law (with significant civil and/or criminal sanctions resulting from a failure to respond or a failure to respond truthfully).

Care is required in responding to any contact from a government investigator (no matter how informal or friendly the contact might seem) because the possible consequences of an inappropriate or careless response are serious. The government may commence an investigation based on information obtained from a variety of sources, including competitors, news reports, premerger notification filings, state agencies, and private litigation.[1] Until the full context of an investigation is

---

[1] Department of Justice, *Antitrust Division Manual III*: 1 [hereinafter AT MANUAL]. The AT MANUAL is available from the Government Printing

correctly understood, an accurate evaluation of the matter or assessment of the wisdom of cooperation may not be possible.

Criminal Investigations. A surprise search warrant is extremely serious and means that the government has a strong suspicion, and probably some evidence as well, of criminal conduct. The DOJ and state attorneys general use search warrants to obtain documents, electronic files and physical items from corporations and individuals for use in a grand jury investigation when there is probable cause to believe that the seized items are evidence of the commission of a crime. Federal Rule of Criminal Procedure 41 governs the procedures for search warrants. The publicly available *AT Manual* describes the circumstances in which the DOJ will use search warrants to gather evidence and procedures relating to their use.

The government also may serve a subpoena for the production of documents or for witnesses to testify before a grand jury. Like a search warrant, a grand jury subpoena is an indication that your company, another company or certain individuals are under investigation for criminal antitrust violations.

Counsel must immediately take charge of the company's response to the government in such criminal investigations. When the DOJ serves a search warrant, a lawyer should go to the site of a search as soon as possible to ensure that the search is properly conducted. He or she should confirm the validity of the search warrant,[2] obtain identification of all of the individuals conducting the search, object if the scope of the

---

Office and, by chapter, in Web, pdf, and WordPerfect formats at www.usdoj.gov/atr/foia/divisionmanual.htm.

2 FED. R. CRIM. P. 41. In general, the search warrant must be validly issued by competent judicial authority, must describe with particularity the property to be seized, state that the property is evidence of a specified criminal offense, provide an exact description of the location to be searched, and note the period of time within which the search is to be executed.

search is beyond that authorized by the search warrant,[3] attempt to list the items being seized,[4] and ensure that company employees are aware of their rights not to answer certain types of questions.[5] The search should not in any way be impeded, as such conduct may constitute obstruction of justice.[6] The government is entitled to seize the originals of documents.[7] As a consequence, the subject of the search must either reach an agreement with the government regarding the handling of the documents and access to them for the purpose of making copies, or must file a motion for return of the documents with the federal district court in the district in which the property was seized. In general, the subject of a search warrant is entitled to reasonable access for such purposes, provided that there are adequate provisions made for the security of the originals.[8]

As with the execution of a search warrant, a grand jury subpoena is an indication that your company, another company, or certain individuals are under investigation for criminal antitrust violations. The following issues must be assessed promptly: (i) the nature and possible targets of

---

3 Items found in plain view that pertain to the criminal investigation may be seized, even if they are not specified on the search warrant. *See* Horton v. California, 496 U.S. 128 (1990) (items found in plain view during a lawful search for other evidence authorized by a valid warrant were lawfully seized).

4 If the scope of the search warrant is broad enough, its execution by the agents may make it difficult or impossible to continue business operations unless immediate access to the items taken is obtained through court order or by agreement with the government. The ability of the subject's counsel to get access to the documents may depend on the thoroughness of the record made during the search of the records seized.

5 A search warrant cannot compel individuals to make statements to the agents. Instead, a grand jury subpoena must be issued and the proper procedures followed by the government before individuals can be compelled to tell what they know about the matters being investigated. FED. R. CRIM. P. 6, 17.

6 *See* 18 U.S.C. § 1503(a) (it is a felony to "corruptly . . . endeavor[] to influence, obstruct, or impede, the due administration of justice").

7 *See* FED. R. CRIM. P. 41.

8 FED. R. CRIM. P. 41(e).

the probe, (ii) possible conflicts of interest arising out of representing the company and individuals, (iii) possible assertion of a privilege by subpoenaed individuals, (iv) whether leniency should be sought for the company or individuals, and (v) communicating with government lawyers regarding the nature of testimony sought and possible immunity.[9]

Civil Investigations. On the federal level, both the DOJ and the FTC have authority to conduct civil antitrust investigations, and both of these agencies have a number of means by which to gather information.

A Civil Investigative Demand (CID) is a precomplaint discovery subpoena issued by the DOJ to obtain information relevant to a civil investigation[10] that can be used in court, before administrative agencies or before a grand jury. A CID recipient may challenge the CID on a variety of grounds, seek to narrow its scope by agreement with the government, or comply without challenge. The FTC similarly can compel the production of information from a company or an individual. There are four types of precomplaint compulsory process that can be issued by the FTC: annual or special reports, access orders, subpoenas, and CIDs.[11]

A request from the DOJ or the FTC for voluntary cooperation in an investigation, including voluntary production of documents and voluntary interviews, also requires careful evaluation by counsel before a decision whether to cooperate is made. The government may not agree to restrict its contact with individuals, even if they are known to be represented by counsel; therefore, early advice regarding the rights of the individuals not to make any statements to the government without careful consideration of the implications and possible risks is essential.[12]

---

9 *See* AT MANUAL, *supra* note 1, providing extensive guidance regarding grand jury procedures and issues.

10 The Antitrust Civil Process Act (ACPA), 15 U.S.C. §§ 1311–1314 authorizes the issuance of CIDs. *See* 15 U.S.C. §1312(a).

11 15 U.S.C. §§ 46(b), 49, and 57b-1(c).

12 *See* 64 Fed. Reg. 19273 (1999), 28 C.F.R. Part 77. "[A]ttorneys for the government shall conform their conduct and activities to" all rules that prescribe ethical conduct for attorneys enacted by the federal local court

Whether the request is an informal request for cooperation, a CID, or some other request, counsel should take certain immediate steps regarding possibly responsive documents. First, counsel should ensure that a statement is issued to relevant company personnel instructing them to preserve all documents (including electronic messages and files) relating to the issues under investigation. Even an innocent destruction of records can have severe consequences. Counsel also should consider whether any documents turned over or copied by the government will divulge trade secrets or other confidential company information if divulged to others. If so, steps should be taken to gain the maximum protection for the documents from inquiries made under the Freedom of Information Act by competitors or litigants in private lawsuits against your company.[13] As stated earlier, counsel should also evaluate the document request with an eye toward negotiating a narrowing of its scope with government lawyers in order to minimize the burden of an overly broad request. Counsel for larger organizations should give special attention to the problem of assuring that all responsive documents have been gathered and reviewed and develop a plan for communicating the request to all business units reasonably likely to have such documents. Follow-up and documentation of the steps taken will be key in these situations.

Counsel must begin gathering information about the subject of the government inquiry. Counsel should interview all company

---

and by the state where the attorney engages in the attorney's duties. 28 C.F.R. § 77.3.

13 15 U.S.C. § 1314(g) exempts documents produced pursuant to a CID from disclosure under the Freedom of Information Act. In responding to other types of government requests for information, counsel may be able to successfully negotiate with lawyers for the government that documents produced will remain confidential. However, it sometimes may be advisable to structure the response to an information request as a formal response (rather than a voluntary submission) in order to get the broadest possible confidentiality protection.

individuals contacted by the government to learn as much as possible about the subject of the inquiry before further steps are taken to respond.

This is particularly so when the inquiry appears to be focusing on the conduct of your company or its employees. Counsel should try to get information about (i) the identity and agency affiliation of the person making the contact, (ii) the general nature of the information sought, (iii) the target of the investigation, (iv) the authority for the contact, and (v) the timing involved in the investigation. In most cases, it will be preferable to have all further contacts managed by counsel for your company. Company employees should be advised that they are under no obligation to provide any information to the government unless and until they are compelled to appear before a grand jury.

Counsel generally should seek to defer an immediate decision on whether to recommend that company employees cooperate with an informal interview request until the full scope of the investigation is understood. This will give counsel time to evaluate whether the company is a target, whether the information possessed by the individuals may be problematic for the company, and whether to recommend that the individuals involved retain separate counsel. Counsel also should locate and review any documents that may appear to have a bearing on the matters under investigation, and assure that any individuals providing information to the government are correctly recalling historical events and their context. Counsel should consider informing the government agency that all current employees are represented by common counsel (inside or outside) and requesting that the government agency make all future contacts through such counsel.[14]

---

[14] Counsel for the company should be careful in assuming that his or her representation should extend to all of the individuals affected by the inquiry. The attorney-client privilege will extend to many of the current employees of the company, but likely not to all. Upjohn Co. v. United States, 449 U.S. 383 (1981). In addition, the interests of the individuals and of the company may not be coextensive, in that the company's interests may dictate a different approach to investigation than if the individuals' interests are exclusively considered. For example, the corporation may be well advised to take steps consistent with the DOJ corporate leniency policy, which could involve bringing matters to the

The businesspeople should be instructed to refer all future inquiries relating to the company and the investigation to designated inside or outside counsel and to advise counsel of any future contact immediately.

Counsel should remain actively involved even if the antitrust authorities profess to need information from the company only as part of an investigation of another company. A government inquiry that targets another company has many business and legal implications. Merely because your company is not targeted by the government does not necessarily mean that the information your company supplies cannot harm your company in the pending investigation, or with respect to unrelated conduct. The information supplied may implicate your company. Moreover, your company's cooperation may prompt a competitor to provide harmful information to the government regarding your company. Counsel also should consider the value to the company of maintaining good relations with the government, especially since the government is usually able to compel a company to provide the information it seeks in any event. Moreover, government investigations can have consequences for a company's future plans. For example, what a company says to the government in response to a proposed merger of two other companies in the same industry as the company can affect the analysis of that company's future merger plans and the legal or fact positions the company might want to take in future transactions of its own. In many (if not most) cases, it will be possible to meet multiple good-faith objectives of the government and the company by negotiating appropriate limits to the scope of document production and by preparing individuals carefully for informal interviews or grand jury appearances.

---

attention of the government that may implicate some employees in criminal activity. *See* DOJ Corporate Leniency Policy (Aug. 10, 1993), *reprinted in* 4 Trade Reg. Rep. (CCH) ¶ 13,113. These potential conflicts of interest warrant careful review because they may affect the ability of counsel for the company to manage the company's contacts both with employees and with the government. *See* ABA SECTION OF ANTITRUST LAW, HANDBOOK ON ANTITRUST GRAND JURY INVESTIGATIONS, 172–75 (2d ed. 2002).

B. "It's just an e-mail to my boss and a few other engineers — nobody outside the company will ever see it, right?"

Discovery in antitrust matters is as broad as in any other legal matter and there are many situations when a client's e-mail or other documents are likely to be seen by people outside the company. Resolution of antitrust issues often is fact-intensive requiring a great deal of discovery. It is not unusual in an antitrust matter for boxes and boxes of many types of documents—correspondence, e-mail, reports, presentations—to be exchanged by the parties or inspected by governmental enforcers. Moreover, the obligation to produce documents in an investigation or litigation applies no matter what form the document takes: formal memo, draft memo, e-mail, documents stored only on computer or backup tape (even if in nonreadable form), audiotape, videotape, notation in a calendar, credit card receipt, cocktail napkin scribble, etc.

Counsel should advise clients on the responsible creation and retention of documents, especially e-mail documents. Document writers should assume all documents will be discovered and reviewed by individuals who are unfamiliar with the industry or, worse, suspicious of the writer's motives. Writers should stick to facts and information they know and avoid speculation or words that can be misconstrued. Writers should be able to explain a document, including why it was created and sent to the recipients, to individuals unfamiliar with (and perhaps hostile to) the company or industry. Writers should be especially careful with e-mail, where the informality might lead some to be less careful in the words they choose. Finally, all company policies for document retention and destruction should be followed.

Once discovery requests are made, counsel should advise clients on the proper retention and collection of relevant documents. Those who reasonably can be expected to possess potentially relevant documents, whether corporate officers or administrative assistants, must be told not to destroy documents until further notice from counsel. Indeed, it is generally advisable to send an e-mail or memorandum to a wider group, advising them of the company's document retention policy, and the need to comply with it. Counsel must search for and produce relevant documents in ways that comply with the discovery request while causing the least interference with the ongoing business. Counsel should document the search and production process to head off any future accusations of noncompliance.

Other discovery issues for counsel in antitrust matters are unlikely to pose issues substantially different from other investigations or lawsuits. Counsel can and should attempt to negotiate limitations on the scope of discovery with the requesting party, whether a governmental investigator or private litigant. Absent agreement, however, courts generally have agreed to a broad scope of discovery in antitrust matters by explaining that the burden of production is outweighed by the need for all relevant information in fact-intensive matters. Courts have allowed broad discovery in terms of relevant time period,[15] geographic area,[16] relevant products,[17] and corporate affiliates.[18] As in other matters, documents that meet the appropriate definition of privilege can be withheld.[19] Finally, courts have been willing to entertain motions for protective orders for confidential information and trade secrets, especially those that strike a balance between the need for secrecy of one party with the need of the other party to properly prosecute a case.[20]

C. "Our international division just called with some legal questions — do they need to worry about antitrust laws too?"

The international division will be subject to the antitrust laws in the countries in which it operates and perhaps to the antitrust laws of other

---

[15] *See, e.g.*, Wilder Enters. v. Allied Artists Pictures, 632 F.2d 1135 (4th Cir. 1980).

[16] *See, e.g.*, Park Ave. Radiology Assocs. v. Methodist Health Sys., 1995-1 Trade Cas. (CCH) ¶ 70,895 (6th Cir. 1995).

[17] *See, e.g.*, Gen. Motors Corp. v. Johnson Matthey, Inc., 887 F. Supp. 1240 (E.D. Wis. 1995).

[18] *See, e.g.*, American Angus Ass'n v. Sysco Corp., 158 F.R.D. 372 (W.D. N.C. 1994).

[19] *See* Upjohn Co. v. United States, 449 U.S. 383 (1981).

[20] *See, e.g.*, In re Indep. Serv. Orgs. Antitrust Litig., 1995-2 Trade Cas. (CCH) ¶ 71,099 (D. Kan. 1995).

countries—including the United States—that are affected by the international division's business activities.

Most nations—including many developing and nearly all developed nations—have antitrust laws (usually called "competition" laws). Over eighty countries have enacted competition statutes and many others are in the process of enacting such laws. These laws are generally similar to the antitrust laws in the United States. For example, most countries have prohibitions similar to those found in Section 1 of the Sherman Act against agreements in restraint of trade, and at least sixty-five countries have enacted premerger notification regimes.[21] Counsel for any multinational corporation is well advised to become familiar with the competition laws of the countries in which his or her company does business.[22]

In recent years, enforcement of antitrust laws has taken on an increasingly international character. The DOJ estimates that well over 90 percent of the total criminal fines it has obtained since late 1996 were from international cartel cases.[23] While enforcement of antitrust laws has

---

21 Douglas H. Ginsburg & Scott H. Angstreich, *Multinational Merger Review: Lessons From Our Federalism,* 68 ANTITRUST L.J. 220–21 (2000).

22 There are a variety of Internet resources available that can assist counsel in becoming generally familiar with the antitrust laws of specific nations and regions. For example, The Asia-Pacific Economic Cooperation (APEC) Web site www.apec.org contains a wealth of information about the competition laws of member countries, which include the United States, Canada, Australia, Japan, the People's Republic of China, Russia, Mexico, and other countries. Information about European Union competition laws can be found at www.europa.eu.int. The Web site of the Organization for Economic Co-operation and Development (OECD), www.oecd.org, contains information about the competition laws of its twenty members.

23 R. Hewitt Pate, Ass't Att'y Gen., Antitrust Div., U.S. Dep't of Justice, The DOJ International Antitrust Program—Maintaining Momentum, Address before the ABA Section of Antitrust Law, 2003 Forum on International Competition Law (Feb. 6, 2003), *available at*

traditionally been a domestic matter, governments are increasingly working cooperatively to enforce antitrust laws. There are a variety of mechanisms that facilitate cooperation. For example, the International Competition Network (ICN) now has sixty-three jurisdictions as members. The objectives of the ICN are to provide support for new competition agencies and to promote greater international antitrust enforcement cooperation and convergence, including the creation of international "best practices" in the merger review process. The Organization for Economic Cooperation and Development (OECD) also has adopted a recommendation that its member countries cooperate to enforce their competition laws.[24] In addition, a number of countries, both within and outside of the European Union, have entered into bilateral agreements that provide, among other things, for information exchanges regarding restrictive practices that may affect the interests of one of the countries. Examples are the cooperation agreements between the United States and the European Commission of 1991 and 1998, which, among other things, permit a party to ask the competition authorities of the other nation to investigate and, if warranted, to remedy anticompetitive activity.[25]

Criminal antitrust violations can result in serious penalties. Recently, competition authorities in the United States and in Europe have levied record fines against companies and individuals and obtained unprecedented jail sentences in connection with international price fixing schemes. In fiscal year 2003, the DOJ filed forty-one criminal cases, and levied more than $107 million in criminal fines.[26]In one recent speech,

---

www.usdoj.gov/atr/public/speeches/2000736.htm [hereinafter *Maintaining Momentum*].

24 *See* The 1995 Recommendation of the OECD Council Concerning Cooperation between Member Countries on Anticompetitive Practices Affecting International Trade, OECD Doc. C(95)130/FINAL 91995.

25 *See* ANTITRUST LAW DEVELOPMENTS (FIFTH) at 1116.

26 *See* Deborah Platt Majoras, Principal Dep. Ass't Att'y Gen. Antitrust Div., U.S. Dep't of Justice, Vigorous Antitrust Enforcement Covering the Waterfront: An Update From the Antitrust Division, Address before the

DOJ Assistant Attorney General Hewitt Pate noted that, in fiscal year 2002, defendants in DOJ criminal cases were sentenced to more than 10,000 days in jail, with an average sentence of more than eighteen months.[27] By fiscal year 2003, the average sentence had increased to twenty-one months.[28]

Activities outside the United States that affect commerce in the United States may be subject to U.S. antitrust laws. The DOJ has made extraterritorial enforcement of U.S. antitrust laws a high priority.[29] The test for whether foreign conduct provides authorities in the United States with subject matter jurisdiction is whether it has a "direct, substantial and reasonably foreseeable effect" on domestic markets or on an opportunity to export from the United States.[30]

As stated earlier, many countries have enacted merger notification regimes similar to the HSR Act. The applicability of these requirements often depends upon the size of the parties or the market share of the parties or both. The Merger Control Regulation of the European Union, for example, applies only to mergers with a "community dimension," which are mergers that meet fairly high turnover thresholds (both worldwide and within the community). There also are variations from jurisdiction to jurisdiction regarding domicile requirements, the definition of relevant markets, and the types of contact that constitutes presence in a jurisdiction. Likewise, the types of information that must

---

State Bar of California, Antitrust and Unfair Competition Law Section, 11th Annual Golden State Antitrust and Unfair Competition Law Institute (Oct. 23, 2003), available at www.usdoj.gov/atr/public/speeches/201435.htm [hereinafter *Vigorous Antitrust Enforcement*].

27 *See Maintaining Momentum, supra* note 23.

28 *See Vigorous Antitrust Enforcement*, *supra* note 26.

29 Daniel G. Swanson, *The Global Reach of U.S. Antitrust Law: 2000 Developments*, ANTITRUST REPORT 17 (Dec. 2000).

30 Foreign Trade Antitrust Improvements Act of 1982, Pub. L. No. 97-290, title iv, § 402, 96 Stat. 1246 (1999), *codified at* 15 U.S.C. § 6a. *See also* ANTITRUST LAW DEVELOPMENTS (FIFTH) at 1116.

be provided also vary greatly among jurisdictions, as do the applicable review periods.[31]

As with American antitrust enforcement agencies, the European Commission has not been hesitant to impose severe penalties on antitrust offenders. The European Commission has broad investigative and regulatory powers to enforce its competition laws, and has imposed significant fines when it has found such violations to have occurred. For example, in 2003 four companies involved in a sorbates cartel were fined a total of 138 million euros.[32] In 1998 fifteen members of a shipping cartel were fined a total of 273 million euros. In 1999, the European Commission imposed a fine totaling 85.5 million euros on eight European and Japanese companies.[33]

Outside the United States and Europe, the adoption and enforcement of competition laws is becoming commonplace. The Canadian antitrust laws are similar to those in the United States. Many Asian nations also have enacted antitrust laws, including Australia, Japan, New Zealand, India, Korea and Taiwan. These laws are in many respects similar to the U.S. regime. Several Latin American countries have antitrust laws on the books as well. Early involvement of skilled counsel conversant with the relevant antitrust laws is critical to assuring compliance with the unique characteristics of local law.

---

31 It is important to carefully review the laws of the specific jurisdictions that may be affected by a merger. The Web site of the International Competition Network includes links to foreign merger control laws. *See* www.internationalcompetitionnetwork.org/mergerscountries.html; see also Michael J. Cicero, *International Merger Control*, 15 Antitrust 15, 16–17 (Spring 2001).

32 *See* Commission Press Release (Jan. 10, 2003), *available at* www.europa.eu.int/rapid/start/cgi.

33 *Id.*

D. "Where can I go for more information?"

A. "Somebody from the Department of Justice (or the Federal Trade Commission or a State Attorney General's office) just called — what should I do?"

- ANTITRUST LAW DEVELOPMENTS (FIFTH) at 674–87, 728–55, 824–34.
- Robert M. Langer, Suzanne E. Wachsstock & Erika L. Amarante, *So You Think You're Safe Under the Antitrust Laws? A Word of Advice to Those Who Would Ignore the States*, ANTITRUST REPORT (Fall 2002).
- U.S. Dep't of Justice, *An Antitrust Primer for Federal Law Enforcement Personnel* (August 2003), *available at* www.usdoj.gov/atr/public/guidelines/201436.htm.

B. "It's just an e-mail to my boss and a few other engineers — nobody outside the company will ever see it, right?"

- ANTITRUST LAW DEVELOPMENTS (FIFTH) at 963–99.
- ABA SECTION OF ANTITRUST LAW, ANTITRUST DISCOVERY HANDBOOK (2d ed. 2003).

C. "Our international division just called with some legal questions — do they need to worry about antitrust laws too?"

- ANTITRUST LAW DEVELOPMENTS (FIFTH) at 1115–1212.
- Ronald W. Davis, *The Mystery Deepens: U.S. Antitrust Treatment of International Cartels*, ANTITRUST 31 (Summer 2003).
- ABA SECTION OF ANTITRUST LAW, COMPETITION LAWS OUTSIDE THE UNITED STATES (2002).

ABA SECTION OF ANTITRUST LAW COMMITMENT TO QUALITY

The Section of Antitrust Law is committed to the highest standards of scholarship and continuing legal education. To that end, each of our books and treatises is subjected to rigorous quality control mechanisms throughout the design, drafting, editing, and peer review processes. Each Section publication is drafted and edited by leading experts on the topics covered and then rigorously peer reviewed by the Section's Books and Treatises Committee, at least two Council members, and then other officers and experts. Because the Section's quality commitment does not stop at publication, we encourage you to provide any comments or suggestions you may have for future editions of this book or other publications.